# THE CLWYD

## LONG DISTANCE TR
## TO CELEBRATE THE MILLENNIUM

### AND TWELVE SHORT CIRCULAR WALKS IN DENBIGHSHIRE, NORTH WALES


**by**
**DAVID HOLLETT**

**Computer design and route marking by**
**BOB READ**



Published by the Ramblers' Association
(North Wales Area)

2nd Floor,
Camelford House,
87-90 Albert Embankment
London SE1 7TW

Ty'r Cerddwyr,
High Street,
Gresford,
Wrexham LL12 8PT

Charity No. 306089

First published August, 2000
with support from the Heritage Lottery Fund
Reprinted June, 2002

Printed by MFP Design & Print, Manchester




**British Library Cataloguing in Publication Data**

ISBN 1-901184-36-6


**All profits from the sale of this publication are to be donated to the funds of the North Wales Area of the Ramblers' Association**

## WELCOME TO THE CLWYDIAN WAY MILLENNIUM TRAIL

The creation of the Clwydian Way fills a gap in Britain's network of Long-Distance Paths. Although more than five hundred such paths are now registered in the country, apart from the Offa's Dyke Path, which passes through north-east Wales, the North Wales Path on the coast, and the shorter, newly-created, Hiraethog & Denbigh Moors Path, (Pentrefoelas to Llanrhaeadr), there is no other Long Distance Path in North Wales which lies to the east of Snowdonia, yet it is universally acknowledged there is no finer rambling country anywhere in Wales.

In the main the path circles round Denbighshire, but in the east it crosses over into Flintshire at two points, and in the west part of the main route up from Corwen, and a considerable part of the alternative, Llansannan route, passes through Conwy County Borough. The entire route, however, runs through what can rightly be termed "The Heart of North Wales" – thus providing long-distance ramblers with a perfect combination of scenic countryside and medieval towns and villages to pass through and enjoy.

To walk the Clwydian Way is to follow in the footsteps of the early, pioneer foot-travellers. Long before Pennant published his famous "Tour" in 1778 this district was well known to many who travelled for health and pleasure. The celebrated Dr. Johnson toured this area in 1774, in company with Mr. and Mrs. Thrale, and Johnson was, in turn, followed by the great rambler and writer, George Henry Borrow. And all these early travellers, it has to be said, passed through a glorious land of song and story, legend, and tales of bygone times.

Above all else though this walk is outstanding because, after leaving Prestatyn, it runs down the Clwydian Range, high above the celebrated Vale of Clwyd, and finally returns through this great valley to its starting point on the coast. The Vale itself actually commences four miles south of Ruthin, then runs for twenty-four miles down to the coast. Enclosed by mountains and moorland these impressive, sometimes brown and barren uplands form a marked contrast to the vivid green meadow-land, far below in the Vale. Towns and villages, great halls, churches, Celtic crosses, cottages and mansions, also lie in this valley, adding variety to the glorious scene. Writing in 1857 William Davis concluded his book on the Vale with these memorable words:-

"Few of us, perhaps in reviewing our bye-gone days, could the hours return again, but would wish many of them differently disposed of, and more profitably employed; but I gratefully say, that that portion I have spent in the contemplation of the romantic beauties of this far-famed Vale, I could by no means wish to recall; they have been, and still are, most conducive to my happiness. To Wales and Welshmen I owe a deep debt of gratitude; and during a residence of a quarter of a century, I have much reason to venerate many warm friends. This work has been compiled with a hope to please Welshmen, and interest Englishmen, and induce some of the latter – I will not conceal it – to visit this splendid Vale, and while they enjoy its beauties, pay off the interest of my debt of gratitude to the inhabitants. I shall then have it in my power to say that I have done some good in my day and generation."

Today, whilst wishing to identify with the spirit of these words, my hope is that this new LDP will not only please Welsh Ramblers, but also encourage walkers from other parts of the British Isles, Continental Europe, and even further afield, to walk in this quite exceptional part of North Wales.

## THE CLWYDIAN WAY – THE ROUTE

This circular, 122 mile long route round Denbighshire, and through parts of Flint and Conwy, was devised to promote rambling and also publicise North Wales. The main route runs from Prestatyn along the Clwydian Range, then on to Llangollen in the south. It then runs west along the Llantysilio range to Corwen, north to Brenig, east through the Clocaenog Forest, and north again, back to Prestatyn.

By the use of an alternative moorland route through Llansannan, and a 'Link Path' near Denbigh, the walk can, however, be broken down into three shorter circular walks, namely, the 88 mile long 'South Clwydian Circular', the 54 mile long 'West Clwydian Circular', and the 42 mile long 'North Clwydian Circular'. Returning via the Mynydd Hiraethog alternative, rather than the main route, adds just two miles to the total distance. For those planning their walk the distances involved are as follows:-

| Section | From – to | Miles |
|---|---|---|
| One | Prestatyn to Tremeirchion | 11 |
| Two | Tremeirchion to Cilcain | 14 |
| Three | Cilcain to Llandegla | 12 |
| Four | Llandegla to Llangollen | 11 |
| Five | Llangollen to Corwen | 13 |
| Six | Corwen to Pentre-llyn-cymmer | 15 |
| Seven | Pentre-llyn-cymmer to Cyffylliog | 14 |
| Eight | Cyffylliog to Trefnant | 15 |
| Nine | Trefnant to Prestatyn | 17 |
| | **Total distance** | **122 miles** |
| Ten | The alternative, Llansannan – Denbigh route | 30 |
| Eleven | The Llangwyfan 'Link Path' | 3 |

## THE SHORTER CLWYDIAN WAY CIRCULAR ROUTES

| | |
|---|---|
| The South Clwydian Circular | 88 |
| The West Clwydian Circular | 54 |
| The North Clwydian Circular | 42 |
| **As three separate walks** | **184 miles** |
| **Twelve short circular walks in or near Denbighshire, totalling** | **65 miles** |

## THE SOUTH CLWYDIAN CIRCULAR – 88 MILES

To walk the South Clwydian Circular, from a point just east of Denbigh, follow the directions in Section 2, from Llangwyfan to Cilcain, all parts of Section 3, from Cilcain, through Sections 4–7 to Cyffylliog, and the first 11 miles of the directions in Section 8. The Link Path (Section 11) should then be taken back to the starting point on the Clwydians at Llangwyfan.

## THE WEST CLWYDIAN CIRCULAR – 54 MILES

To walk the West Clwydian Circular, from Pentre-llyn-cymmer in the south, follow all the directions in Section 7, to Cyffylliog, the first 11 miles of Section 8, to Denbigh, and all the 'anti-clockwise' directions in Section 10, back to Pentre-llyn-cymmer, just south of Llyn Brenig.

## THE NORTH CLWYDIAN CIRCULAR – 42 MILES

To walk the North Clwydian Circular follow all the directions in Section 1 from Prestatyn, to Tremeirchion, the first 8 miles of Section 2, from Tremeirchion to Llangwyfan, then take the 'Link Path', Section 11, westbound, to the banks of the Clwyd, just to the west of Glan-y-Wern farm. Turn north at this point and follow all the Directions in Section 8.3 and all of the directions in Section 9 back to Prestatyn.

## TWELVE SHORT CIRCULAR WALKS IN OR NEAR DENBIGHSHIRE

In the second section of this guide we have included route descriptions of twelve short circular walks in, or near Denbighshire, all of which are based on a particular section of the main Clwydian Way. These will appeal to those who like moderate, rather than long distance walking. They also give those who are considering walking the complete route an opportunity to get a 'taste' of this long distance path before committing themselves to the full trek. (Using a two-car system, with one vehicle at the beginning and the other at the end of a short section, the main orbital route/s could, of course, be walked with ease by less able walkers, unable or unwilling to 'back-pack' – and from one central accommodation base!)

## FORWARD PLANNING

The main and secondary routes have an excellent main-line rail connection at Prestatyn, where the main walk begins and ends. The main walk is, however, a long one so do plan well in advance. If you are an experienced rambler allow about 12 miles a day – or even more with light summer evenings. At this rate those who are planning to walk round the full circuit should allow about ten days, but in your plans do try to allow time to explore Denbigh, Ruthin, Llangollen, Corwen, and St. Asaph, as all these ancient Denbighshire towns have so much to offer the visitor. You will also need up-to-date copies of Denbighshire County Council's accommodation and information leaflets which are obtainable from the Tourist Information Centres listed on the following page.

## WHAT TO CARRY

What gear you take depends on the season, but good quality walking boots and waterproofs are absolutely essential at all times of the year. A compass, maps and a first aid kit should also be carried and, if you have a mobile phone take it with you. Keep to a minimum what you take, but do be aware, there are no shops on the path between Corwen and Ruthin on the return section of the main route, and between Corwen and Llansannan on the Mynydd Hiraethog alternative route, although on this section there are several good pubs, and at the Visitor Centre at Llyn Brenig there is a cafe.

## PROBLEMS ON THE ROUTE

The route is not 'Waymarked' but is easy to follow. The Highways Departments of Denbighshire County Council, Conwy County Borough Council and Flintshire County Council have all co-operated in this project, each one indicating that they would do their utmost to ensure that the entire route is clear and usable by January, 2000. However, if you do encounter any problems please contact the local authority concerned, as listed below:-

### DENBIGHSHIRE

The Rights of Way Manager
Denbighshire County Council
Caledfryn
Smithfield Road
Denbigh LL16 3RJ
(Tel: 01824 706871)

### FLINTSHIRE

Director of Transport & Planning
Flintshire County Council
Rights of Way Section
County Hall
Mold CH7 6NR
(Tel: 01352 752121)

### CONWY

Highways & Technical Services
Conwy County Borough Council
The Heath, Penmaenmawr Road,
Llanfairfechan LL33 OPF
(Tel: 01492 574000)

## TOURIST INFORMATION CENTRES

The friendly staff at the Tourist Information Centres in Prestatyn, Rhyl, Ruthin Llangollen, Corwen and Mold have much information on attractions, accommodation – hotels, B&B's, camp sites etc. – also local eating places, entertainments, and places to visit, and will be only too pleased to help you enjoy your walk around North Wales.

### PRESTATYN

Prestatyn Tourist Information Centre
Offa's Dyke Interpretative Centre
Central Beach, Prestatyn
Denbighshire LL19 7EY
(Tel: 01745 889092)

### RHYL

Rhyl Tourist Information Centre
Children's Village
West Promenade
Rhyl, Denbighshire LL18 1HZ
(Tel: 01745 344515/355068)

## RUTHIN

Ruthin Tourist Information Centre
The Craft Centre, Park Road,
Ruthin, Denbighshire LL15 1BB
(Tel: 01824 703992)

## LLANGOLLEN

Llangollen Tourist Information Centre
Town Hall, Castle Street,
Llangollen, Denbighshire LL20 5PD
(Tel: 01978 860828)

## CORWEN

Corwen 'One Stop Shop'
Corwen
Denbighshire LL21 0DR
(Tel: 01490 412378)

## MOLD

Tourist Information, Mold Library,
Museum & Gallery, Earl Road,
Mold, Flintshire CH7 1AP
(Tel: 01352 759331)

## LOGGERHEADS, DENBIGHSHIRE (FOR COUNTRYSIDE INFORMATION)

Loggerheads Countryside Centre
Loggerheads Country Park,
Loggerheads,
Nr. Mold,
Denbighshire CH7 5LH
(Tel: 01352 810614)

## THE CLWYDIAN RANGER BUS SERVICE

The Clwydian Ranger is a network of Sunday and Bank Holiday scenic, recreational bus services to and within the Clwydian Range AONB which are designed to offer car-free access to this lovely area of countryside. The Ranger network enables visitors and local people from Wirral, Merseyside, Deeside, Wrexham, Rhyl, Prestatyn or Llangollen to catch one of the buses to an outward point on a trail, including many sections of the Clwydian Way and also the Offa's Dyke Path, and walk back without having to retrace one's steps. All the Clwydian Ranger bus services meet and interchange at Loggerheads Country Park and Countryside Centre, making it the perfect place to change buses for other scenic routes. For further details please ring 01352 704035 or 01824 706968

## ACKNOWLEDGEMENTS

I would like to thank the following organisations and institutions for their help and co-operation relating to various aspects of this project:- The Ordnance Survey; Denbighshire County Council; Conwy County Borough Council; Flintshire County Council; The Environment Agency; Hyder Utilities (Operations) Limited; Welsh Water; North-West Water; University of Liverpool Library; The British Library; Central Libraries at:- Denbigh, Mold, Birkenhead and Liverpool.

Also Bob and Tina Read for some of the photographs and the following members of the Ramblers' Association, who accompanied me on the survey of this route and/or read the draft document:- Mary Robinson, RA Executive; Margaret Fernley, Chairman, North Wales Area RA; Pete Bland, North Wales Area General Secretary; John Robinson; Colin Yarwood, North Wales Area Treasurer; Ron Williams, Secretary, Flintshire Footpath Committee; Donald Rooksby, Conwy Footpath Committee; Dereck Shoreman and Rhys Roberts, Cerddwyr Edeyrnion Ramblers; Frank McKecknie, Vera Laurenson, Brian Bevan, Eddie Owen, Angela Osborne, Linda Jones,

Brian Hughes, Maureen Dittmer, Maurice & Brenda Depledge and Bill Neill, Wirral Group, Ramblers' Association; John Mather, Brenda Taylor, Vera Hollett and Roger Cox, Rainbow Ramblers; Cyril Jones, Mel Williams and Frank L. Brown of the Denbighshire Footpath Committee; Neville Fernley, Conwy Footpath Committee RA, and John Arwel Watkins, R.A. Policy Officer, Wales.

**David Hollett**
**Secretary, Denbighshire Footpath Committee, March, 2000.**

**THE RAMBLERS' ASSOCIATION**

The North Wales Area of the Ramblers' Association covers the six unitary authorities of North Wales, from Anglesey to the Whixall Moses near Whitchurch and from the north coast to Dolgellau. The wild country of Snowdonia is world famous but the more subtle landscapes of the Denbigh Moors, the Clwydian Hills and the Vale of Clwyd are much less well known. There are riches here and Dave Hollett's guide to the route he has opened up with the aid of Denbighshire County Council and called the Clwydian Way, reveals those riches, both scenically and historically. Dave Hollett is secretary of the Rambler's footpath committee for Denbighshire and members of that committee and from the Wirral Group of the Merseyside & West Cheshire Area, have assisted in the path surveying. Enquiries about the work of the Ramblers' Association should be made to our Welsh Office, Ty'r Cerddwyr, High Street, Gresford, Wrexham LL12 8PT, Telephone 01978 855148

**John Robinson**
**Retiring North Wales Area General Secretary, December, 1999.**

# THE CLWYDIAN WAY

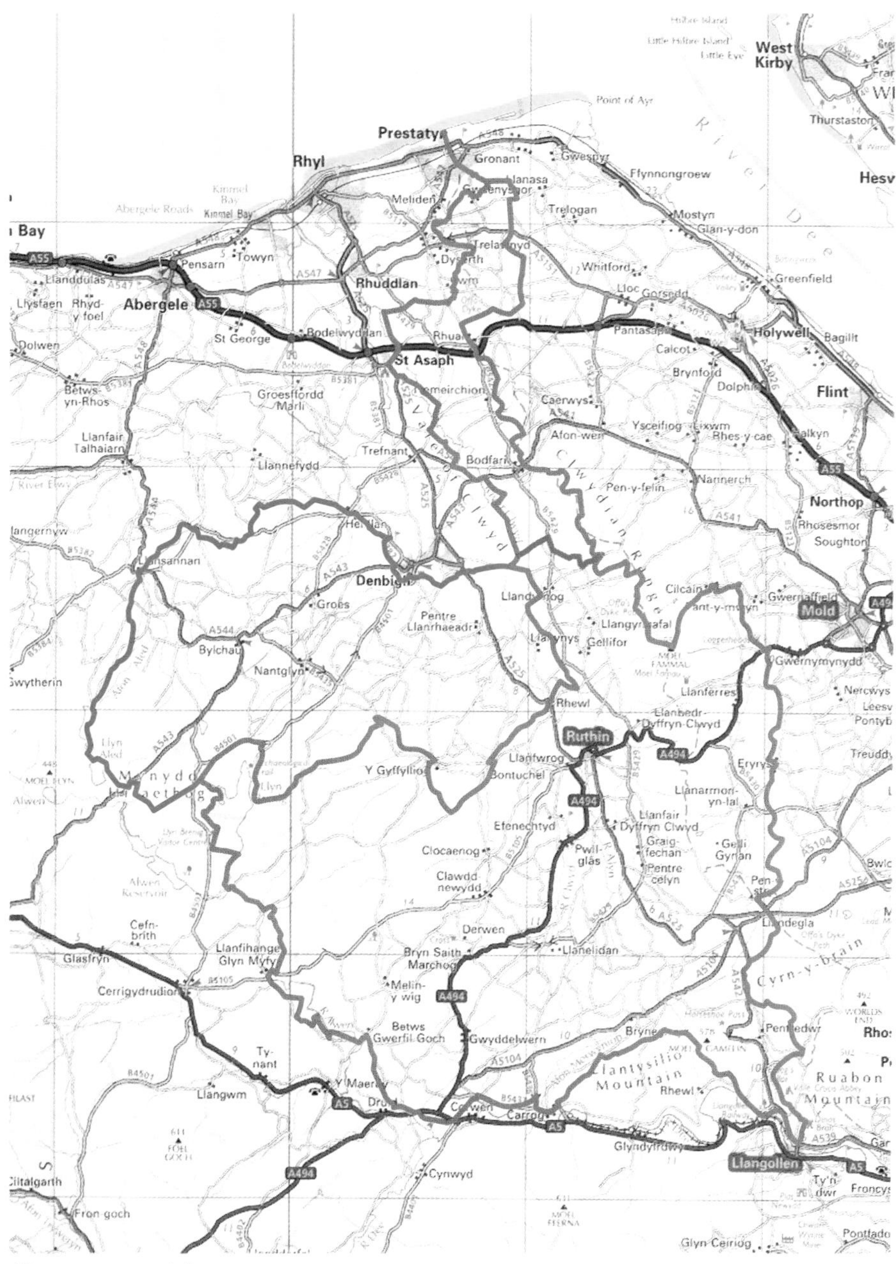


Crown copyright

Main route marked in purple; Llansannan route marked in red; 'Link Path' marked in green.

| Maps Required: OS Pathfinder series:- 771. 737. 755. 772. 773. 787. 788. 789. 805. 806. OS Explorer series:- 264. 265. 256. 255. |
|---|

## Section 1. Prestatyn – Tremeirchion. 11 miles. (1.1. Prestatyn – Trelawnyd.)

**The route.** From the sea front at Prestatyn go past the main line railway station (1) at the north end of High Street. From this point proceed south east down High Street, which continues as Fforddlas, up to the 'T' junction at Mount Ida Road and Bishopswood Road. Turn right here into Bishopwood, then first left into Hillside, which continues as Prestatyn Road to Gwaenysgor. Climb up the hill, round the sharp bends for just under a quarter of a mile to SJ074821.

Take the footpath on the left here, which soon crosses a lane, then continues east past St. Elmo's Summer House. At SJ090819 turn right, taking the path which runs south-east, past Golden Grove (2) to a lane at SJ094811. Turn right here keeping Talfryn Woods on the left up to the road junction at SJ091811. Turn left and continue south on this lane to the footpath on the right at SJ091805. Continue south up the eastern side of Gop Hill.

On Gop Hill (3) one can leave the main route, at the sign post, and proceed to the Cairn and view-point on the summit, before rejoining the main path and continuing south to the lane at SJ091801, which is just to the north of Trelawnyd. Turn right here and continue south to the A5151 which is in the centre of the village at SJ091797.

**(1) Prestatyn and the Holyhead Railway.** Built to secure fast communications with Ireland, the Chester & Holyhead Railway was also primarily responsible for securing the rapid development of Prestatyn, Rhyl, Colwyn Bay, Llandudno and Bangor into flourishing resort and residential towns. The link between Chester and Bangor was opened on 1 May, 1848. In days gone by there was a Prestatyn castle, which has virtually disappeared. Originally a Welsh fortress that the English captured, Prestatyn was then strengthened and enlarged. Today, the famous Offa's Dyke Path begins/ends at this famous resort town.

**(2) The 'Fighting Morgans' of Golden Grove and St. Elmo's Summer House.** Like a notable Crusader of nearby Gwaenysgor, the 'Fighting Morgans' of Golden Grove used the Saracen's hand as their badge. During the Commonwealth the Morgans were staunch opponents of Oliver Cromwell. One of the most outstanding features of the old Morgan estate was St.Elmo's Summerhouse (SJ085818) which is now just a ruin, but its foundations are thought to stand on the remains of a Bronze Age Barrow. On a clear day the views from this high vantage point are spectacular, for places as far apart as Kirkudbright in Scotland, Ireland, Derbyshire and the Isle of Man, are visible.

**(3) The great tumulus on Gop Hill.** The large stone tumulus on the summit of Gop Hill (SJ086801) can be seen dominating the plateau for many miles around. In spite of its fame and prominence it is not possible to give a date or explanation for its construction. In the 19th century, mainly due to the historical theory of Edward Parry of Chester, the tumulus was romantically named 'Boadicea's Tomb'. On a clear day the views from this famous hill are also spectacular.

## Section 1. Prestatyn – Tremeirchion. (1.1. Prestatyn – Trelawnyd)

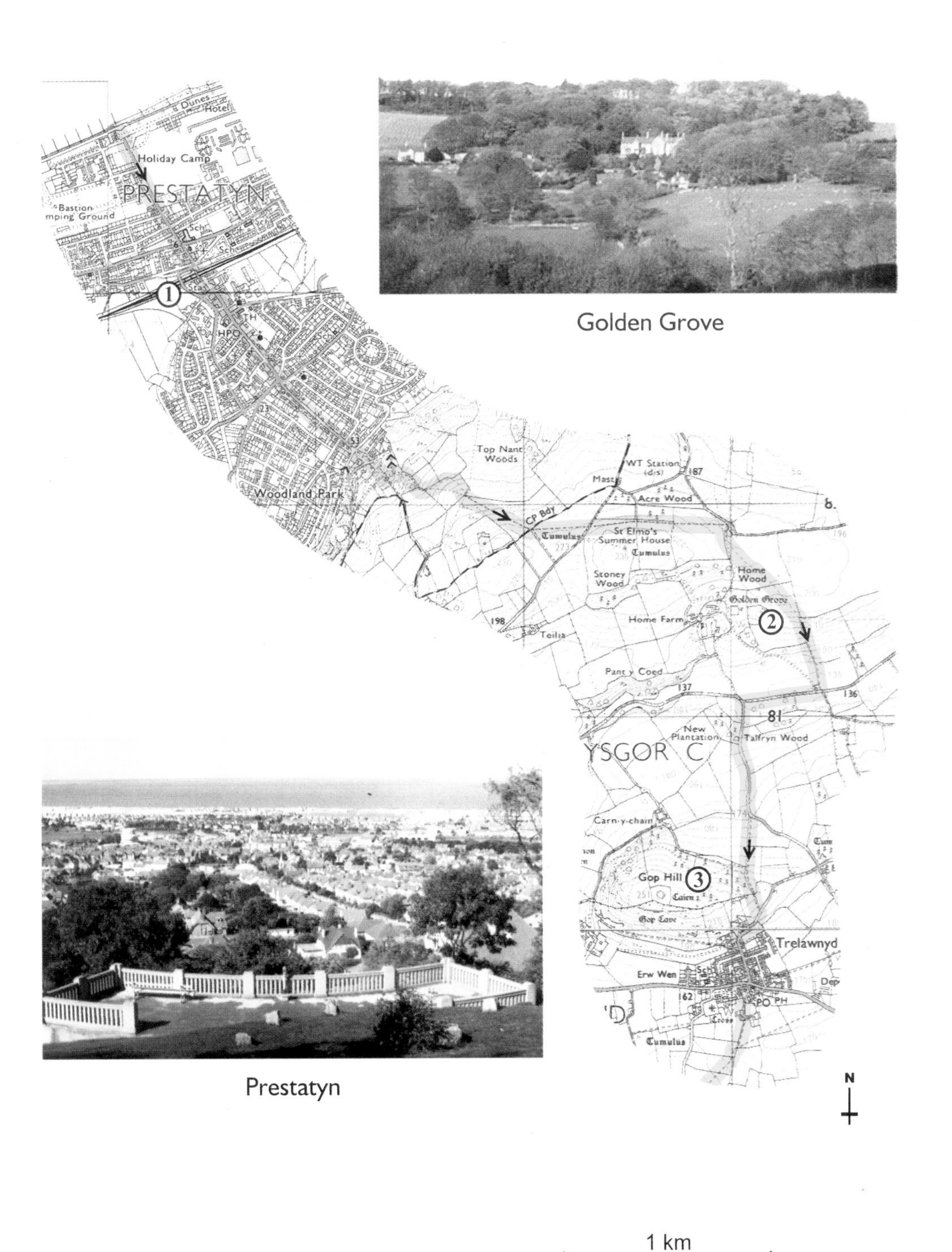


Golden Grove

Prestatyn

**Section 1. Prestatyn – Tremeirchion. (1.2. Trelawnyd – Coed Jenny Morgan)**

**The route.** At Trelawnyd (1) cross over the A5151 and take the path opposite as outlined on the map to Graig-Arthur. Now turn south, take the path through the wood known as The Flash, and on to the lane at SJ095775. Cross over the lane here and continue south on the path until it reaches another lane at SJ096772. *

Continue south, past Hendre-fawr Farm, and on to the lane at Tynewydd, SJ094764. Cross over the lane and continue south-west, below Coed Jenny Morgan to the next lane at SJ092762. Turn right, continuing west along the lane below Coed Jenny Morgan, past the cross-roads, and on to the north-east end of a short section of the Offa's Dyke Path at SJ085765. Take this path south-west to the next lane.

* If the path is blocked at this point take the alternative route highlighted in orange on the strip map.

**(1.1) Trelawnyd – the village of many names.** Trelawnyd, located just to the south of Gop Hill, was only renamed as such in 1954. The village has also been known as Rywlfnwyd, Trelofnid and Trelofnewyd in its time. In 1700 an enterprising local businessman changed the name to Newmarket – in order to promote the market he had established there. The village expanded with the lead mining in the area, largely based on the 'Golden Grove' and 'Talar-goch' pits, between the late 17th and mid 19th centuries.

**(1.2) Trelawnyd, Suetonius Paulinas and Queen Boadicea.** In A.D. 60 the Roman Governor Suetonius Paulinas moved north to conquer Anglesey. He succeeded, but in doing so almost lost the larger island of Britain itself! Whilst thus engaged the whole of south-east Britain rose in revolt under the leadership of Boadicea. Paulinas rode south with his cavalry, well ahead of his main force, to find and subdue the 'rebel' forces. About the final battle between the Britons and the Romans Tacitus wrote: 'It was a glorious victory, like those of the good old days. Some estimate as many as 80,000 British dead. There were only 400 Romans killed, and scarcely more wounded'.

But precisely where this decisive battle was fought remains a mystery. In 1850 the historian Edward Parry of Chester published his celebrated work – 'Royal Visits and Progresses to Wales' in which he argued that the carnage took place in the joint parishes of Caerwys, Newmarket, and Llanasa in Flintshire! Today, mainstream historians suggest various places, further to the south, but the battle has been sited as far afield as Chester by the German Scholars Mommsen and Domaszewski.

## Section 1. Prestatyn – Tremeirchion.
## (1.2. Trelawnyd – Coed Jenny Morgan)

The tumulus on Gop Hill

1 km

1 mile

## Section 1. Prestatyn – Tremeirchion. (1.3. Coed Jenny Morgan – Tremeirchion)

**The route.** At the lane near Brynllithrig Hall turn left and continue south to Rhuallt on the B5429 Tremeirchion/Bodfari Road, which then passes under the A55 Expressway. At Ty Gwyn (SJ077745) take the footpath on the left (north-east) side of the road. This path winds up the hill, then bears left until it crosses another footpath at Maen Efa. Turn right here, heading south to the lane just to the north of St. Beuno's College at SJ081743. (1) Cross over the lane and continue south behind the college, to the junction of this path with another at SJ082741. Head due east on this path until it reaches the Offa's Dyke Path at SJ085741. Continue south for a few hundred yards on the ODP then, at SJ085740, turn right and head south down the lane to Ty Cerrig at SJ083738 Turn left here, taking the path south-east then south to Tremeirchion (2) near the Salusbury Arms.

**(1) St. Beuno's College and Gerard Manley Hopkins.*** St. Beuno's College, a Jesuit foundation, was built in 1848 by the Victorian architect, Joseph Aloysius Hansom (1808–82). It was here that the poet, Gerard Manley Hopkins (1844–1899), lived for three years, 1874–1877, studying theology in preparation for the priesthood. A convert to Catholicism, he burnt all his early poetry when he converted, but was persuaded to write again by the rector. Unfortunately, the poem he wrote was rejected by the Jesuit magazine! In fact, his work was not published until 1912, thirty years after his premature death from typhoid fever at the age of 45. Today he is respected throughout the world as one of the great 'Nature Poets'. Inspired by the beauty of the Vale of Clwyd, on 19 June 1876, he wrote 'Moonrise' – part of which reads:–

> I awoke in the Midsummer not–to–call night, in the white
>         and the walk of the morning:
> The moon, dwindled and thinned to the fringe of a fingernail
>         held to the candle,
> Or paring of paradisical fruit, lovely in waning but lustreless,
> Stepped from the stool, drew back from the barrow, of dark
>         Maenefa the mountain.

( Moel Maenefa is the hill directly behind and east of St. Beuno's College. )

**(2) Tremeirchion.** Tremeirchion, originally 'Din Meirchion', the fortress of Meirchion the chieftain, is an attractive village overlooking the wide expanse of the Vale of Clwyd. The old church between the village school and the inn, has an 800 year old yew tree in the grounds, while in the church lies a mail–clad knight of about 1280, shown cross–legged and drawing his sword. Most impressive of all – by the altar stands the great canopied 14th century tomb of Madog – 'Black David' the Teacher of Hiraddug.

* Please note. St. Beuno's Ignatian Spirituality Centre is a 'Silent Retreat'. Accordingly, staff are not available to escort casual visitors around the Centre. However, the College and the famous 'Rock Chapel' – on the summit of a hill in the college grounds, are both visible from nearby lanes and paths.

## Section 1. Prestatyn – Tremeirchion.
## (1.3. Coed Jenny Morgan – Tremeirchion)

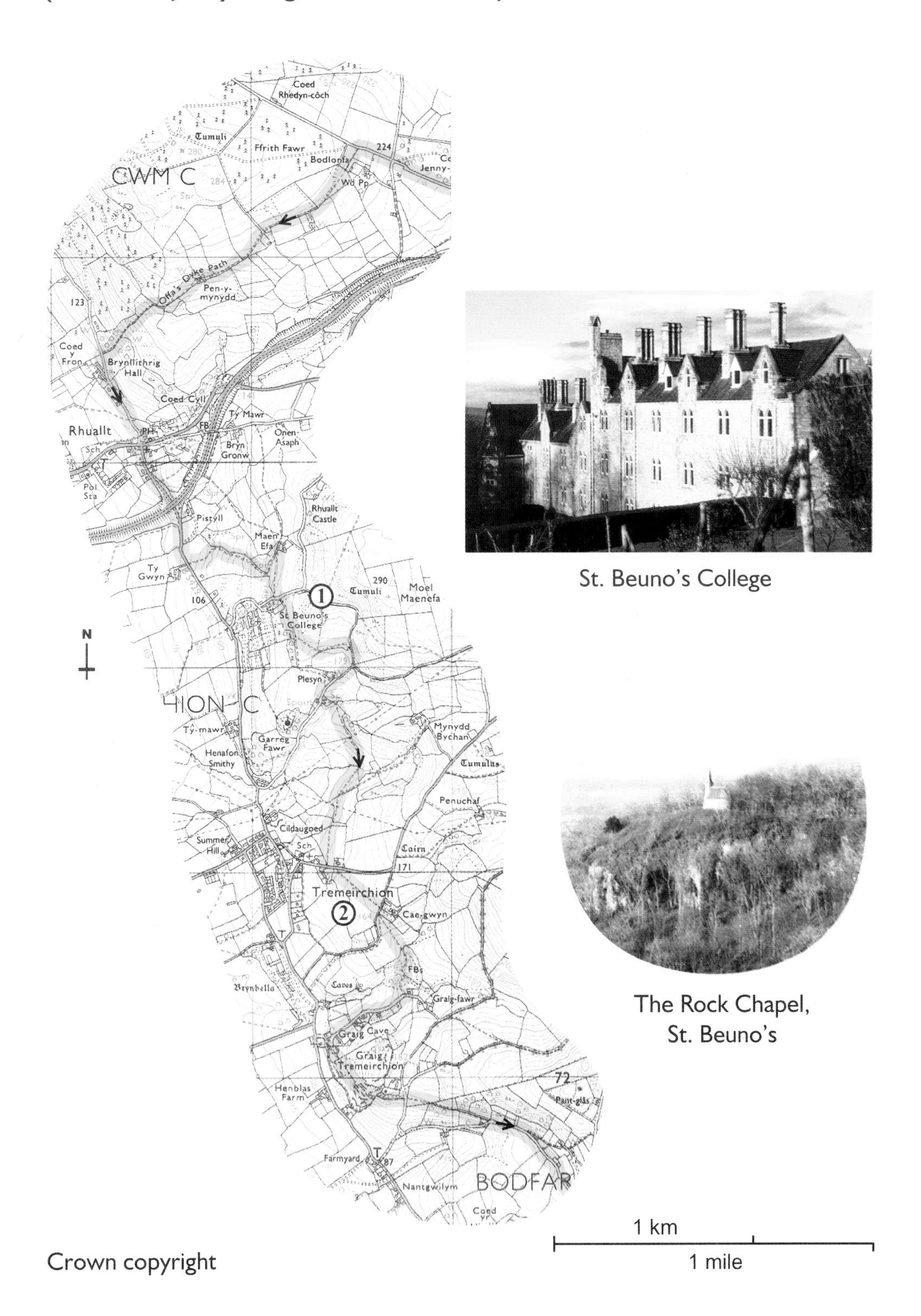


St. Beuno's College

The Rock Chapel, St. Beuno's

## Section 2. Tremeirchion – Cilcain. 14 miles. (2.1. Tremeirchion – Fron-gelyn)

**The route.** At the Salusbury Arms, Tremeirchion, turn left and continue up the road to Bryn Farm Now take the path on the right which runs south-east to Cae Gwyn (SJ086728). This path continues south until it reaches the lane just to the west of Graig Fawr. Now head south-west down the lane to SJ084721, which is just to the north of the Graig Tremeirchion Nature Reserve, near 'Brynbella' (1).

Turn left taking the footpath through the Reserve to the lane at SJ087719, then continue on the same path to another lane at SJ092718. Bear left, and continue down the lane to the cross-roads. Turn right here, and continue down the hill to the 'T' junction at SJ096712. Turn right and continue south-west down the lane to 'Plesyn' at SJ092709. Turn left up the drive, and climb over the stile which is on the right-hand side. Continue round the grounds of 'Plesyn' then take the path which runs just south of Moel-y-Gaer Fort (2) and down to the lane at SJ097704. Turn right taking the lane down to Bodfari (3) at SJ092701. Cross over the A543 and head south to a lane at SJ097701. Now follow the lanes as indicated, past Grove Hall, then follow the path/bridleway to SJ121690. From here take the bridleway to a point just above Fron Gelyn at SJ124674.

**(1) 'Brynbella' Tremeirchion.** At the south end of Tremeirchion stands the great mansion of 'Brynbella'. It was designed by the architect C. Mead and built between 1792 and 1795 for Dr. Johnson's friend, Mrs Thrale, and her second husband, Gabriel Piozzi, an Italian music teacher. Mrs Thrale was born Hester Lynch Salusbury, daughter and heiress of John Salusbury of Lleweni. The celebrated traveller, Dr. Johnson was introduced to the Thrales in 1764. Henry Thrale M.P. was a prosperous Brewer, and M.P. for Southwark from 1768–1780. Johnson soon became almost a member of the Thrale family. The corpulent Doctor commenced his celebrated journey into Wales on 5 July, 1774, in company with Mr. and Mrs Thrale, and their daughter who subsequently became Lady Keith.

**(2) Moel-y-Gaer hillfort, Bodfari.** This hillfort, at SJ095708, is the lowest of many such establishments on the Clwydian range. Nevertheless, it commands a fine position above the valley, which enabled the occupiers to control access into and from the Vale of Clwyd. It is cleverly defended by a double circuit of ramparts on the naturally weak west side, whilst the very steep slopes away to the east made any further man-made defences quite unnecessary.

**(3) Bodfari.** It was once suggested that Bodfari could be the Varis of Antonio – Bod - Vari, or a township belonging to the Roman station Varis. Today, however, it is not thought to be the case by many academics who now think that St. Asaph is a far more likely location. The famous Dinorben Arms, the lychgate together with the church itself, with an early 19th century house – Hafod Tan Eglwys – form a most picturesque group in this delightful Welsh village. High above, and just to the south of Bodfari, the giant TV mast on Moel y Parc now dominates the surrounding area.

## Section 2. Tremeirchion – Cilcain.
## (2.1. Tremeirchion – Fron-gelyn)

Brynbella, Tremeirchion

The lychgate, Bodfari

Crown copyright

## Section 2. Tremeirchion – Cilcain. (2.2. Fron-gelyn – Cilcain)

**The route.** From Fron Gelyn continue along the bridleway until it reaches the lane just to the east of Llangwyfan (1) at SJ130664. (This point marks the east end of the 'Link Path'.) Turn left here, following the lane round a RH bend for a short distance to SJ131664. Now take the bridleway on the right, which contours round the hill until it reaches another lane just south of Moel Arthur at SJ141656. Turn left here, taking the lane up to the foot of Moel Arthur (2) at SJ147657. Now head south, taking the Offa's Dyke Path to the summit of Moel Famau (3) at SJ161626. From the Jubilee Tower take the path heading north-east down to the outskirts of Cilcain then continue up the lane to the centre of the village at SJ177652.

**(1) Llangwyfan.** This beautiful village has a special, more recent claim to fame. During the early decades of the 20th century the most common cause of death in Wales was tuberculosis. A fund was set up to build a special hospital at Llangwyfan to treat this complaint. The opening in 1920 was to be remembered for many years, for the ceremony was performed by George V accompanied by Queen Mary. By the 1950's advances in medical science led to a considerable decline in the number of patients. In 1975 threats of closure led to a massive campaign to save this famous hospital. Nevertheless, it eventually closed in 1982, but subsequently became a residential community run by a mental health charity.

**(2) Moel Arthur.** Just to the east of Llangwyfan, high on the Clwydian range, Moel Arthur is a small but prominent hillfort. The northern defences consist of two enormous banks and ditches. In 1962 a notable hoard of Early Bronze Age copper flat axes was found within this fort. According to legend Moel Arthur is also the place where Arthur buried a crock of gold!

**(3) Moel Famau.** The remains of the Jubilee tower, on Moel Famau, are the highest point on the Clwydian Range at 1818 ft (554 m). This mountain was formerly the property of the Crown, but was purchased by the late Lord Kenyon, one acre on its summit, and a road up to it having been reserved. In 1809, George I I I reached the fiftieth year in his reign. A public subscription paid for the tower to commemorate the Golden Jubilee of George's reign. A great storm in 1862 reduced the impressive Egyptian style monument to the ruins that you can see today. The views from the summit are very extensive and varied. The Vale of Clwyd can be seen from end to end, and on a clear day it is also possible to see places as far away as Rivington Hill, Snowdonia, Cumbria, and the Isle of Man. (Today, the summit of Moel Famau is jointly owned by Flintshire and Denbighshire County Councils)

## Section 2. Tremeirchion – Cilcain. (2.2. Fron-gelyn – Cilcain)

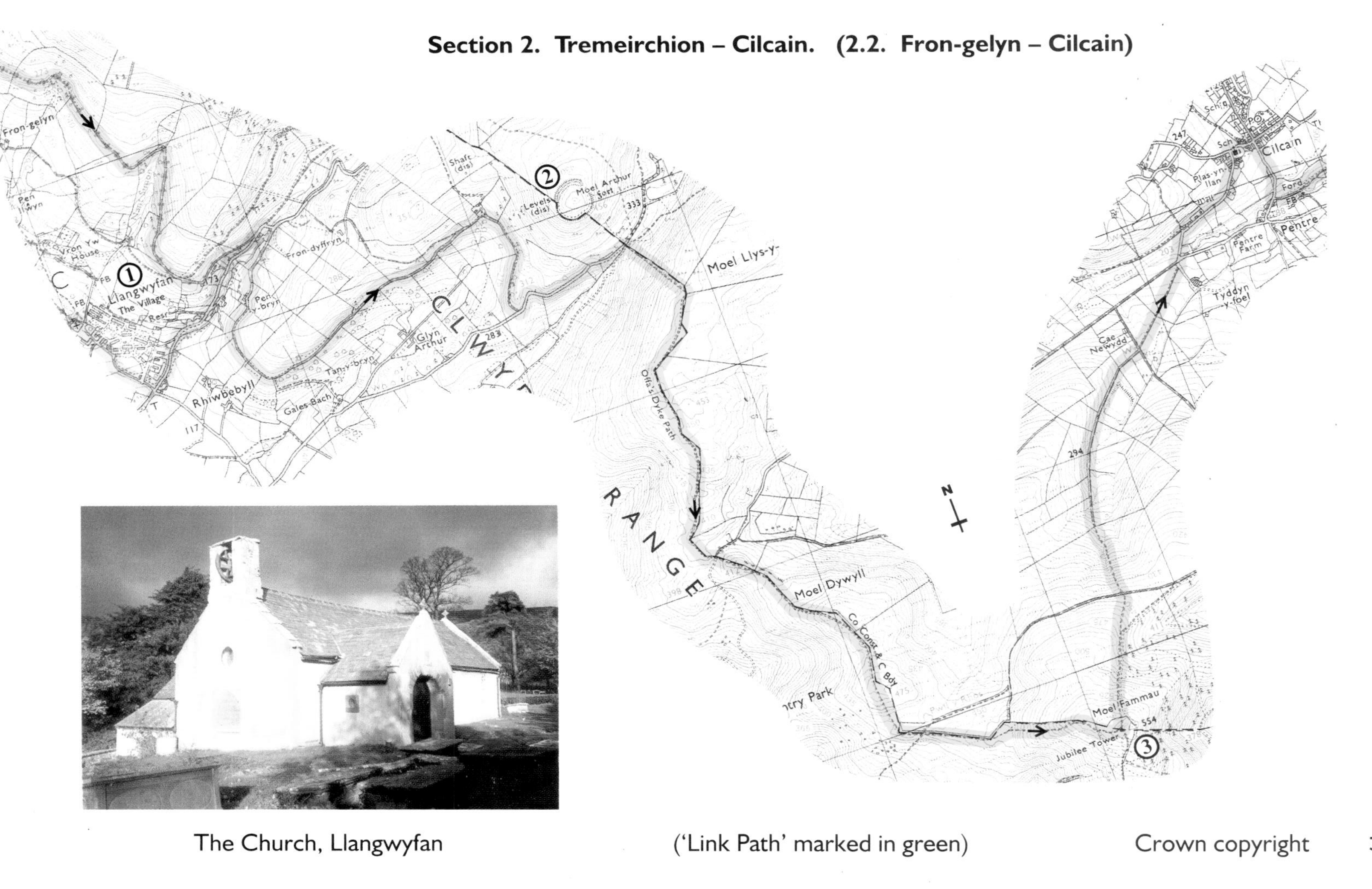


The Church, Llangwyfan

('Link Path' marked in green)

**Section 3. Cilcain – Llandegla. 12 miles. (3.1. Cilcain – Maeshafn)**

**The route.** From Cilcain (1) take the lane south towards Pentre. After a short distance, at Sj177649, take the path on the left to the lane above the Afon Alun. Go straight on down the hill, over the bridge, then up the hill to the path on the right at SJ189652. This is the famous Leete Path, which runs through the Alun Valley (2) to Loggerheads (3) on the A494. From Loggerheads take the A494 up the hill towards Mold for a quarter of a mile to SJ202626. Cross over the road here, then take the track/footpath which loops through the grounds of the Colomendy Centre for Outdoor Education (4) until it reaches SJ201621 at the south side of the Centre. From this point continue along the path to the lane just to the west of Maeshafn. Bear left here, continuing up the hill to the centre of the village. (5)

**(1) Cilcain.** Cilcain means 'a beautiful place of retreat' and is mentioned in the Domesday Book. The name derives from the 6th century when Eurgain, the niece of Saint Asaph and wife of Elidir, hid in a cave near the village. The Parish Church of Cilcain is dedicated to St Mary the Virgin. The present church dates from the 14th century although many alterations and additions have been made over the years. In the village there was no mains water supply until 1904, consequently all drinking water had to be carried from St. Mary's Well near White Cottage.

**(2) The Alun Valley.** In places the famous 'Leete Path' runs along the cliffs, high above the Afon Alun. Today the Leete appears as a dry ditch. In the days when this now peaceful valley was the scene of extensive lead mining activity a total of four 'Leetes' carried water to enormous water wheels, which in turn pumped water from the mines to prevent flooding. The powerful Grosvenor family, of Eaton Hall, Chester, first showed an interest in mining in the area when they purchased a lead-smelting mill at Mold in 1601, but it was only after the Restoration, in the 1660's, that large-scale mining commenced, which continued in Flintshire well into the 20th century.

**(3.1) The 'We Three Loggerheads Inn'.** The following extract from a paper presented to the Cosmopolitan Society tells the story behind the name of this pub:- "In explanation of the name 'Loggerheads' the following anecdote was interesting. The story ran that a vicar of Llanferres quarrelled with some man in the parish and both eventually agreed to meet at the Inn to settle differences. Unfortunately they agreed to disagree, and made the breach between them larger still. So Richard Wilson, the celebrated artist, who lived with his aunt, Mrs Catherine Jones, Colomendy, painted portraits of them knocking their heads together and he gave it the title 'We Three Loggerheads' the observer of the sign making up the third party."

**(3.2) Mendelssohn and the Alun Valley.** The great German Composer Mendelssohn also has a most interesting link with the Alun Valley! In 1829, when staying with John Taylor, a mining engineer of Rhydymwyn, near Loggerheads, he composed 'The Rivulet'.

## Section 3. Cilcain – Llandegla. (3.1. Cilcain – Maeshafn)

Lead miners at work

Mendelssohn, 1834

White Horse Inn, Cilcain

1 km

1 mile

**(3.3) Merseyside and Crosville at Loggerheads.** In 1927 the sons of the founder of the Crosville Motor Company purchased two fields and a wood at Loggerheads for £1600. A tea house was built, and in the summer Crosville buses carried thousands of Merseysiders out to this much-loved beauty spot from their terminus at Woodside Ferry, Birkenhead. Unfortunately, right up to 1939, the accounts on this project showed a small loss every year, but it was money well spent for the bus traffic that it brought to the Company. During the 2nd World War the tea house was used to store tinned pilchards! Eventually the estate was bought by the old Clwyd County Council, and it is now owned and managed by Denbighshire County Council.

**(4) Liverpool and the Colomendy Centre for Outdoor Education.** The Camp School at Colomendy was one of many planned and built by the National Camps Corporation because of the threat of war in 1938. These camps were to be used for evacuation in wartime and for holidays in peacetime. Leased back to various city authorities – in this case Liverpool – it served as a 'Country School for City Children', giving urban youngsters an insight into rural life. Colomendy opened in 1939, just in time to house children evacuated from Liverpool during the blitz. In 1956 Liverpool Corporation acquired Colomendy for £46,500. Since it became an Environmental Studies Centre, up to 1994, three hundred and fifty thousand Liverpool children have passed through this famous establishment.

Autumn Tints, Loggerheads

**(5.1) Maeshafn – the village.** The great Maeshafn Lead Mine was established about 200 years ago. In the early years of the 19th century it closed. On reopening in 1823 this small mining community enjoyed a boom period in the middle years of the century. Appropriately, the popular pub in the village is called The Miners' Arms. According to its inscription the Chapel was built in 1820, and enlarged twice, once in 1843 and again in 1863.

The Miners Arms, Maeshafn

**(5.2) Maeshafn and the International Youth Hostel Movement.** The National Youth Hostel organisation was formally established in March, 1930. By Christmas of the same year the first hostel was in operation at Pennant Hall, in the Conwy valley. By Easter 1931 four hostels were opened in North Wales, which included two on the route of this Long Distance Path. One was the Old School House at Cyffylliog beyond Ruthin, the other was the 'Pilkington' Hostel at Plas-yn-Cornel, Llansannan. Then in July, 1931, the first purpose-built hostel was opened; this was the Holt Hostel at Maeshafn. Weatherboarded Neo-Georgian, with pediments and shutters, it was designed for the Y.H.A. by the celebrated architect and creator of Portmeirion – Sir Clough Williams-Ellis.

The Youth Hostel, Maeshafn

## Section 3. Cilcain – Llandegla. (3.2 Maeshafn – Graianrhyd)

**The route.** From the centre of Maeshafn take the lane which runs south past the Miners' Arms. After a few hundred yards this lane becomes a footpath. Keep on this path which continues to the south until it reaches a lane at Pant-du. (SJ205594). From here take the path opposite which contours up and over the hillside then leads down to the road on the west side of Eryrys. From the village take the road that runs south towards Llanarmon-yn-Ial. After going down the hill, and round the 'Z' bend, at SJ201571 turn left and follow the path due south along the limestone ridge down to the B4530 Ruthin Road, which is just below Craig Quarry, at a point one mile west of Graianrhyd.

Eryrys

## Section 3. Cilcain – Llandegla. (3.2. Maeshafn – Graianrhyd)

Maeshafn

1 km
1 mile

## Section 3. Cilcain – Llandegla. (3.3. Graianrhyd – Llandegla)

**The route.** From the B4530 below Craig Quarry take the lane directly opposite which runs up the hill to the Transport Yard at Creigiog Ucha. Take the path on the right which goes round the side of the yard then runs south to the golf course at SJ202550. Turn left here, pass through the yard at Allt Gymbyd farm, then continue along the lane to a path on the right at SJ208548. Take this path which runs south-west to Bod Idris Hall Hotel. Pass through the hotel grounds, then continue south down the tree-lined drive to a sharp bend at SJ206533. At this point continue straight ahead, following the path which winds round the east side of Pen-y-Bryn, and on to Llandegla. (1)

(1) Church of St. Tegla and St. Tegla's Holy Well. The church of St. Tegla, Llandegla, was entirely rebuilt in 1866, but retains its old font. It is named after St. Tegla, a 2nd century female Turkish saint who was a disciple of St. Paul. Quite how this saint came to be honoured in Denbighshire remains a mystery. Nevertheless, her well at Llandegla subsequently became famous for healing epilepsy! Sufferers performed a strange ritual which involved bathing in the well, sticking pins in a chicken, and sleeping under the church altar, whilst at the same time clutching the unfortunate bird. The epileptic fits were thus transferred to the chicken which then obliged by stumbling about to confirm the miraculous cure. Not surprisingly, the church authorities condemned these performances, but they continued until about 1813.

Church of St. Tegla, Llandegla

## Section 3. Cilcain – Llandegla. (3.3. Graianrhyd – Llandegla)

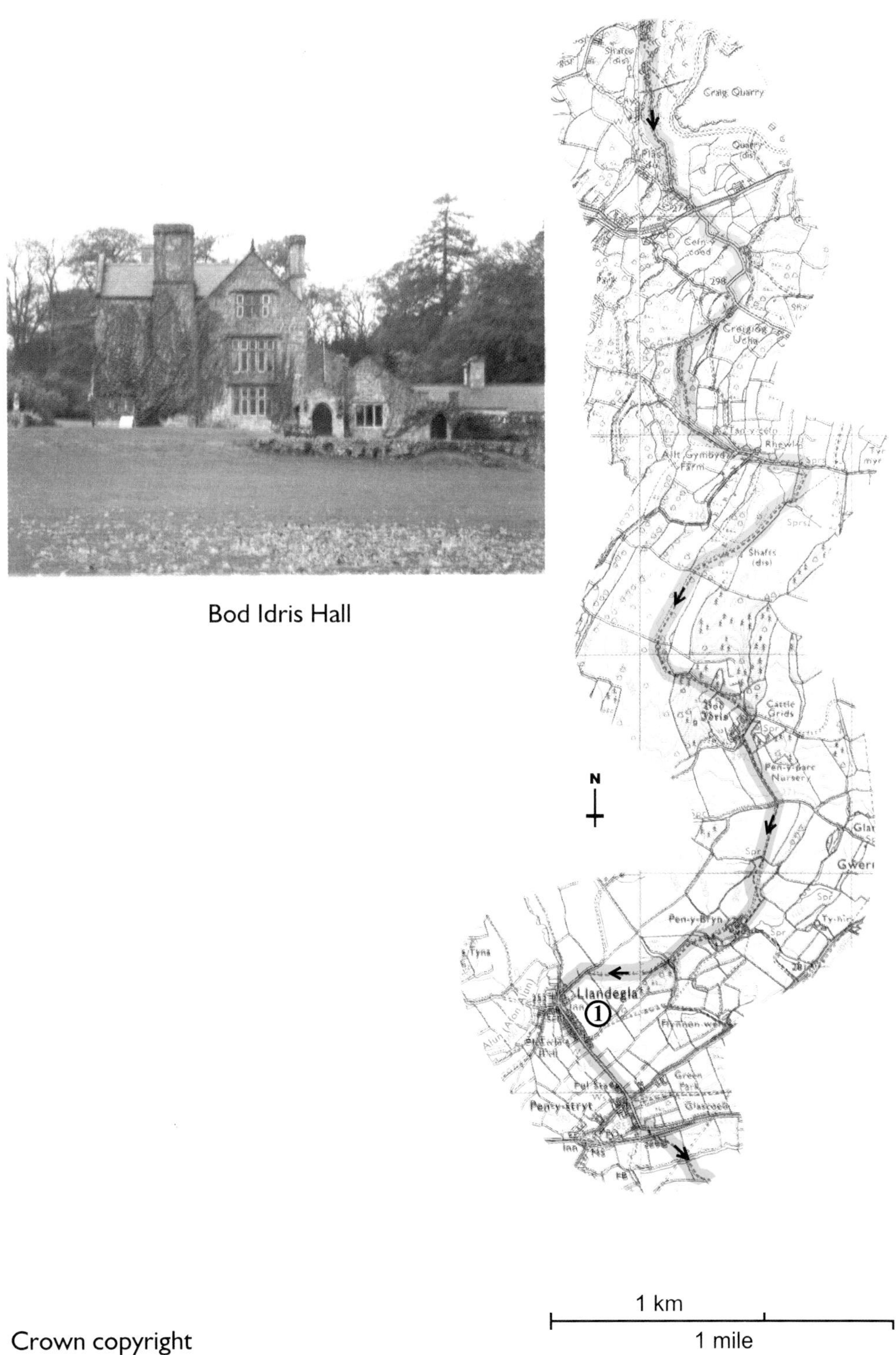


Bod Idris Hall

**Section 4. Llandegla – Llangollen. 11 Miles. (4.1. Llandegla – Eglwyseg Glen)**

**The route.** From Llandegla follow the Offa's Dyke Path south for about 1 mile to Hafod Bilston at SJ207512. From here take the gated county road south-west, past Graig Farm, Faraway and Pentre Isaf to SJ193496 on the A542 Llangollen road. Turn left, and head due south for 1 mile, to the Ponderossa Cafe, which is situated at the head of the world famous Horseshoe Pass. Here turn left, taking the minor road down the hill for a few hundred yards to a gate at SJ193481. This point marks the west end of a spectacular path which heads east then south, past Bryn-yr-odyn, Cae'r-hafod and Glyn, before reaching the lane junction at Plas Yn Eglwyseg, Eglwyseg Glen. From this path walkers will have splendid views over to World's End, (1) at the head of this great valley, the Eglwyseg Rocks, and the famous old Manor House (2) at SJ229479.

**(1) World's End.** World's End is the name given to the head of this beautiful valley which lies below the impressive line of the Eglwyseg Rocks. On the high limestone plateau which stretches away above these great cliffs are a number of Bronze Age barrows and cairns. The Offa's Dyke path now contours along this hillside, on the opposite side of the valley, just below the cliffs, taking walkers directly south towards Llangollen.

**(2) The Old Manor House.** Plas Uchaf (or Manor House) World's End, was once owned by Colonel John Jones, supporter of Cromwell, and one of the Regicides who suffered on the scaffold at the Restoration. The main house is usually assigned to 1563, but it is of more than one date – the wing clearly being much older. It was to this place, previously Prince Cadwgan's hunting lodge, that his son Prince Owain brought Princess Nest. At some point in 1135 Owain and other Welsh princelings returned from exile in Ireland. Whilst away their various sisters became wards of Henry 1. One of them, Nest, daughter of Rhys ap Tewdr, became the King's mistress.

Henry then married off Nest to Gerald, Earl of Pembroke. At Christmas, 1135, Owain met and fell in love with Nest, so abducted her, together with her children! Back in his father's hunting lodge at Eglwyseg the impulsive young prince then planned to enlist all the disaffected Welsh into a country-wide war. Cooler heads talked him out of this ill-conceived venture, and to ensure peace Henry offered Owain a place in his army – where he could learn to become a worthy Knight! Peace then returned to the Hunting Lodge at Eglwyseg. The highly adaptable Nest then made her way south, married Stephen Constable, and raised a large family.

## Section 4. Llandegla – Llangollen. (4.1. Llandegla – Eglwyseg Glen)

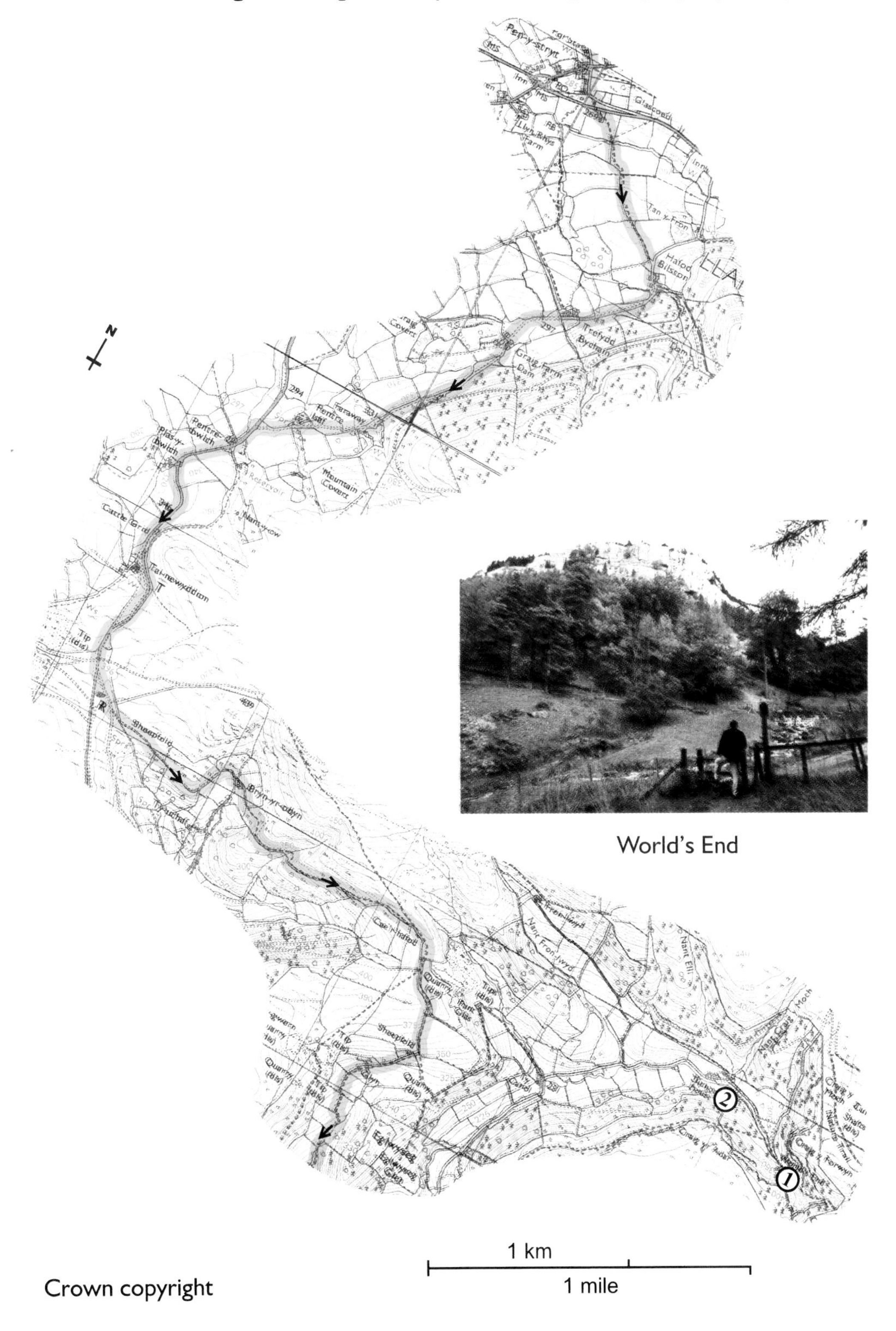


World's End

## Section 4. Llandegla – Llangollen. (4.2. Eglwyseg Glen – Llangollen)

**The route.** Continue south down the lane, around the sharp bend at Plas Yn Eglwyseg to SJ215460. Turn right here taking the footpath which runs to the west past Eglwyseg Mill and on to Tan-y-Fron at SJ208458. Turn left and continue round the back of the farm for about 100 yards to the next path on your right. Take this path south to Abbey Cottage at SJ205447. Bear right here if you wish to view Valle Crucis Abbey (1) or left if you want to continue south on the main route, which will soon bring you to the lane to the south of Bryn-hyfryd at SJ213436. Continue down the lane to the 'T' junction, then turn left and follow the lane round for a quarter of a mile to a footpath on the left, by a stream, at SJ215432, which heads due east to Castell Dinas Bran. (2) Follow this path to SJ218431, turn left here taking the path round the north side of Dinas Bran to SJ226432. Now take the path to the summit of Dinas Bran, then continue down the well-marked path to the bridge and railway station at Llangollen.

**(1) Valle Crucis Abbey.** The famous Valle Crucis Abbey near Llangollen was founded in 1201 by Madoc ap Gruffydd, a grandson of Owain Gwynedd. It was built for the white-robed Cistercian monks whose custom and practice directed that they settle in such isolated places. The Order was originally richly endowed with lands and privileges. In the abbey is displayed a collection of monuments to local Welsh nobles, which includes a sculptured slab of Madoc, great grandson of the founder and great-grandfather of Owain Glyndwr. Within the Abbey is reputed to be the last resting-place of Iola Goch, a landowner in the valley and the celebrated bard of Owain Glyndwr.

After the suppression of the abbey by Henry VIII the site of Valle Crucis and the surrounding lands passed to Sir William Pickering, and after various changes Valle Crucis Abbey became part of the Coed Helen Estate, the trustees of which conveyed the abbey ruins to the Ministry of Works in 1950 for permanent preservation under the provisions of the Ancient Monuments Acts.

**(2) Castell Dinas Bran, Llangollen.** The great fortress of Castell Dinas Bran, whose ruins still crest the hill to the north of Llangollen, date back to the 13th century. Established by the Welsh Lords of Powis, it was abandoned to the forces of Edward I in 1277. Quite probably the home of Gryffudd ap Madoc, son of the founder of Valle Crucis Abbey, over the years Dinas Bran passed through powerful hands – including those of the Fitzalans and Myddletons. According to legend it is also one of the many places that King Arthur is said to have placed the Holy Grail. Today, the hill and fortress are owned by Denbighshire County Council.

## Section 4. Llandegla – Llangollen. (4.2. Eglwyseg Glen – Llangollen)

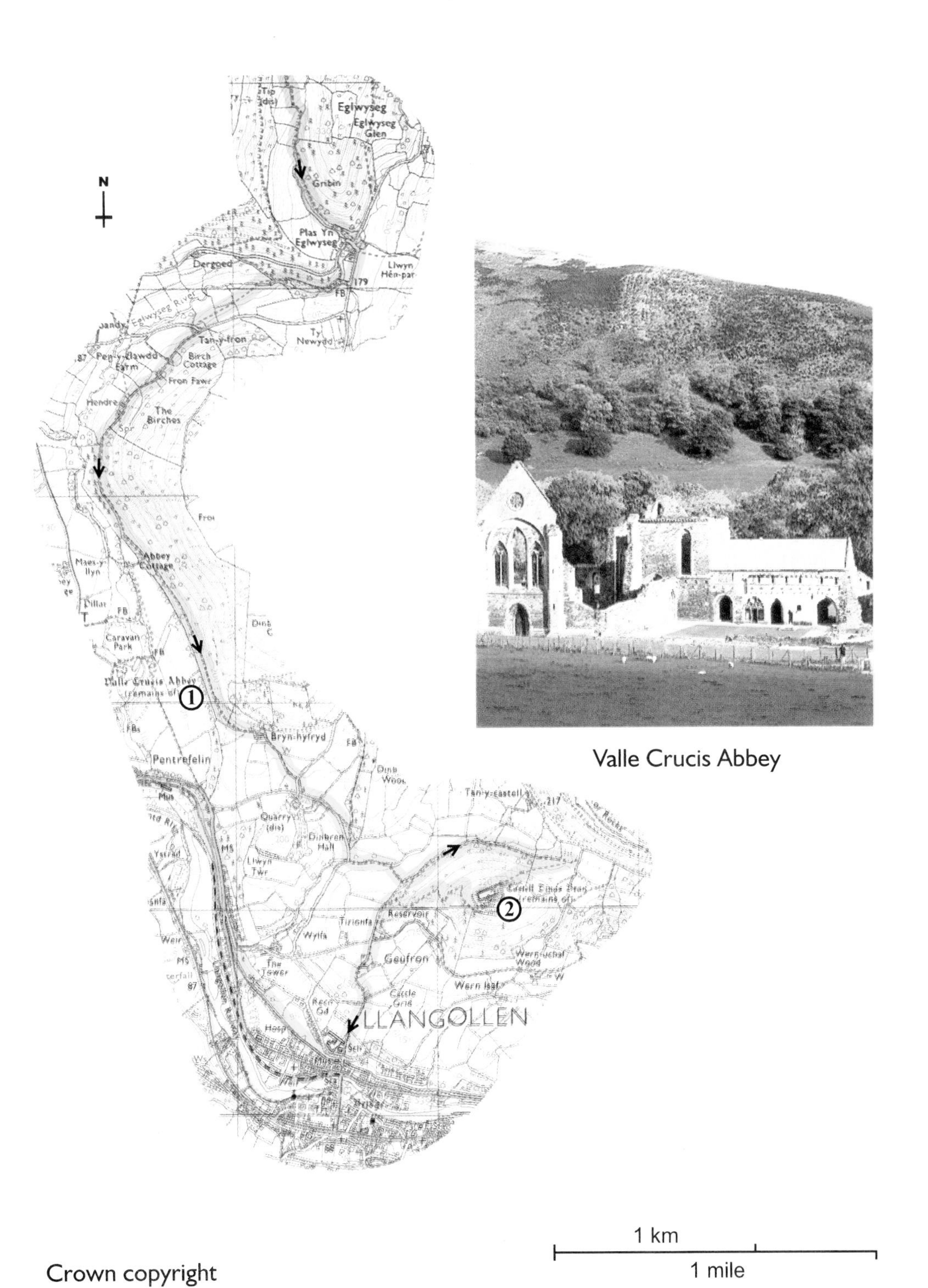


Valle Crucis Abbey

## Section 5. Llangollen – Corwen. 13 miles. (5.1. Llangollen – Rhewl)

**The route.** From Llangollen (1) take the canal tow path to the north-west then west, for about 4 miles, passing the Chain Bridge Hotel and the Horseshoe Falls, until the path joins the secondary road leading to Rhewl. Head north-west on this road to the junction by Llidiart Annie at SJ190444, then proceed up the lane to Llandyman at SJ187450. Turn left here, taking the path down to Rhewl at SJ183449.

**(1.1) Llangollen.** Llangollen, the town which is now famous throughout the world for its annual International Musical Eisteddfod was so named from the dedication of its church to an ancient British Saint named Collen. In 1852 The Hand, The King's Head and Royal Hotel were the three principal Inns. The population at this time stood at 1,500. In the late 19th century the town was celebrated for the superiority of its flannel fabrics, and Llangollen Ale, both invaluable products then being well-known throughout Britain. In the late 18th and 19th centuries the town was an important staging point on the London–Holyhead road.

**(1.2) The Bridge.** The great stone bridge over the Dee at Llangollen consists of four pointed arches. Traditition ascribes a bridge over the Dee to John Trevor, Bishop of St. Asaph, in the mid 14th century, but one almost certainly existed before this time. The present structure probably dates from about 1500. It was, in days gone by, regarded as one of the wonders of Wales. It was widened in 1873, and again, almost a century later, in 1968–69.

**(1.3) The Llangollen Railway.** The first sod of the Vale of Llangollen Railway was cut by Colonel Tottenham, the Vale of Llangollen chairman, on 1 September, 1859. Construction was then carried out by the great railway contractor, Thomas Brassey of Birkenhead. The Llangollen & Corwen Railway was incorporated by an Act of 6 August 1860, with Tottenham as chairman. The line finally reached Corwen in the autumn of 1864. Today, a short stretch of the line is in operation between Llangollen and Carrog, but there are plans in hand to extend it to Corwen.

**(1.4) By charabanc from Liverpool to Llangollen.** Llangollen, it is interesting to note, was the destination of the world's first charabanc trip in 1906. This pioneering vehicle was chartered by 18 adventurous members of the Liverpool Bowling Club.

**(1.5) Plas Newydd.** On the south side of the town is Plas Newydd – the now half-timbered house of great but uncertain age, which was the famed retreat of Lady Eleanor Butler and Miss Ponsonby, better known as 'the two recluses of Llangollen'. For half a century, from about the year 1788, they lived graciously and entertained widely, but at the same time regarded their magnificent home as 'a retreat from the frivolities of fashionable life'. Nevertheless, Wordsworth, the Duke of Wellington and Sir Walter Scott feature on a long list of decidedly fashionable celebrities who were entertained by the 'recluses' at their pleasant retreat!

## Section 5. Llangollen – Corwen. (5.1. Llangollen – Rhewl)

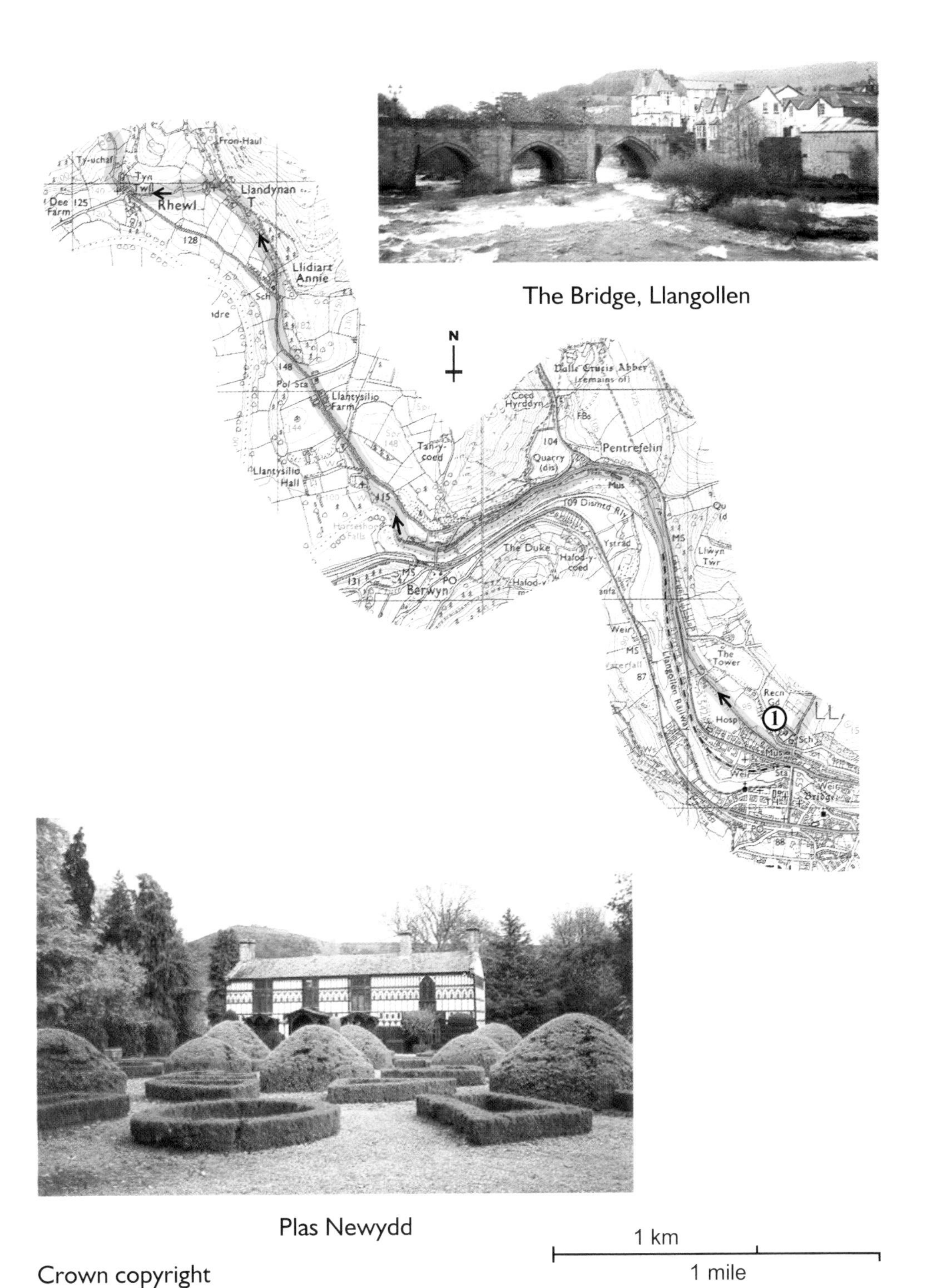


The Bridge, Llangollen

Plas Newydd

## Section 5. Llangollen – Corwen. (5.2. Rhewl – Nant-y-madwen)

**The route.** From the village at Rhewl, at SJ183449, take the side lane which heads north-west up the Llantysilio Mountains, above Glyndyfrdwy (1) which lies in the Dee Valley, to the south, at SJ150427. At SJ176456 the signposted track (county road) should be taken to the top of the ridge between Moel y Gaer and Moel y Gamelin (SJ171465). From this point bear left, WNW down the hill, to the point where the path joins the bridleway at SJ159469, to the east of Bryneglwys. (2) Contour west along this bridleway for about 2 miles, to the lane at SJ131457, which is just south of Blaen Yale Farm. Now take the next bridleway, which continues past the ruins of Nant-y-Madwen at SJ126451, en route to Carrog.

**(1) Glyndyfrdwy and Owain Glyndwr.** It was at Glyndyfrdwy that Owain Glyndwr had one of his two great mansions and estates, the other being at Sycharth, south of the Berwyn Mountains. Born about 1359, he later entered the Inns of Court to train as a barrister. Whilst there he attracted the attention of King Richard II. He then served with distinction in the wars in the retinue of Henry of Lancaster and in the Scottish campaign of 1385.

When Henry IV ascended the throne Owain was living quietly at Glyndyfrdwy, although at loggerheads with his neighbour, the litigation enthusiast, Lord Grey of Ruthin. Ironically, the dispute was over the ownership of a small strip of relatively worthless moorland. It was at this point that the King called upon Glyndwr to attend him in the Scottish War. Unfortunately, the message was entrusted to Grey, who deliberately failed to deliver it. Understandably, the King was angry with Glyndwr, and Glyndwr with Grey for maliciously scheming to present him as a traitor.

In September, 1400, realizing his arrest was imminent, Owain took action. His friends gathered in Glyndyfrdwy and then marched on Lord Grey's town of Ruthin, which they burnt to the ground. The war had begun, and it was to continue for over a decade. The last big raid organised by Glyndwr came in 1410 when his forces swooped in Shropshire. But they were beaten; Rhys the Black, Philip Scudamore and Rhys Tudor were executed. No one knows for sure what happened to Glyndwr, but it seems likely that he spent his last days at Monnington Manor, in the Golden Valley of Hereford, sheltered by his son-in-law John Scudamore. Twice the new king, Henry V, offered the rebel leader a pardon, but the old man was apparently too proud to accept.

**(2) Bryneglwys and Yale University.** Two miles to the north-east of Bryneglwys, on the north side of the A5104 (SJ173491) is Plas-yn-Yale – a modest grey stone manor house which was the ancestral home of the Yale family. It was the birthplace of the Pilgrim Father David Yale who settled in New Haven, Connecticut, in 1637. His son, Elihu Yale, was born in America, but returned with his parents to Britain at the age of four. He then made a fortune in India, out of which he provided funds for a college to be founded at New Haven, which was named Yale University in his honour.

**Section 5. Llangollen – Corwen.**
**(5.2. Rhewl – Nant-y-madwen)**

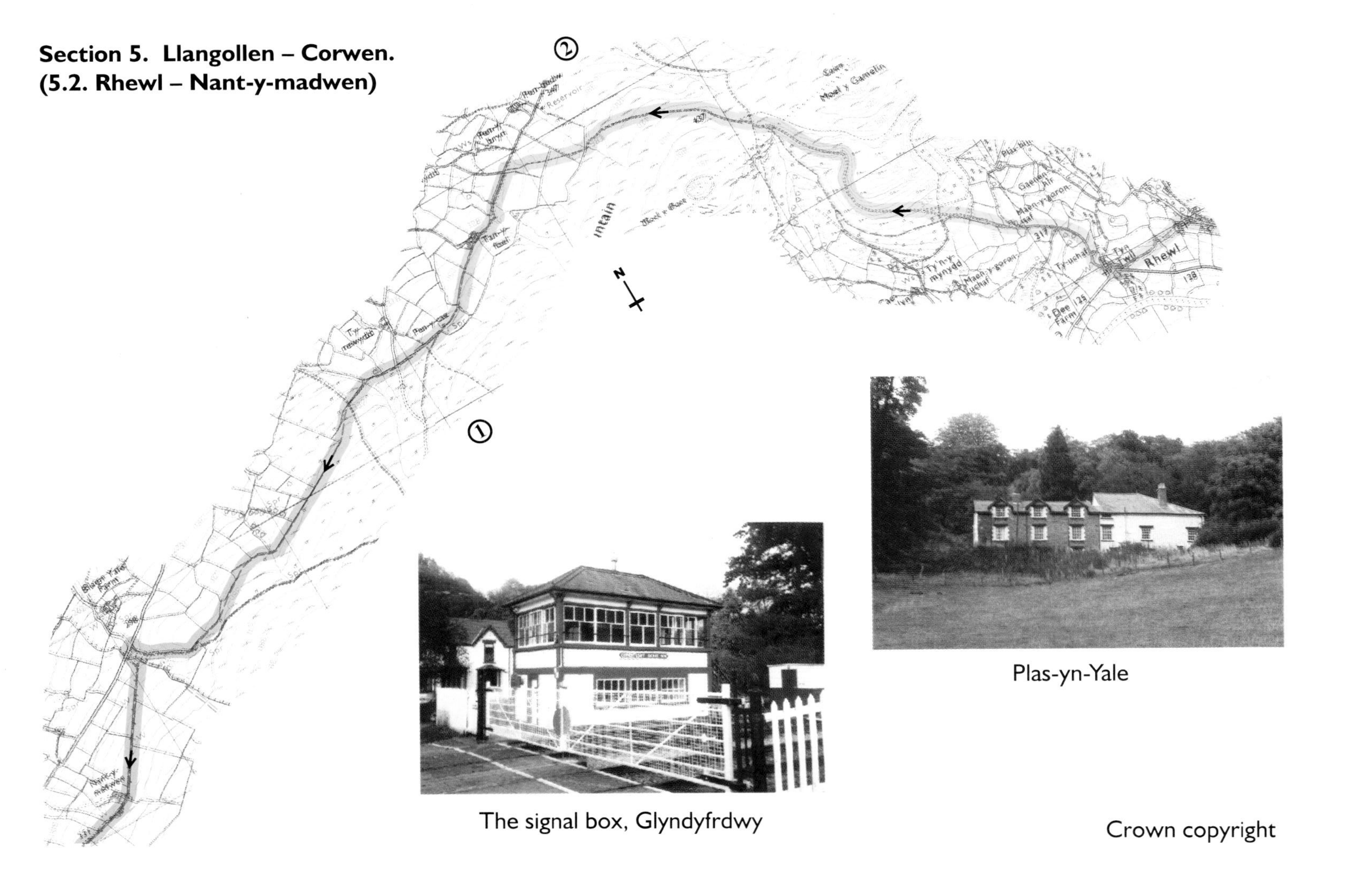


The signal box, Glyndyfrdwy

Plas-yn-Yale

## Section 5. Llangollen – Corwen. (5.3. Nant-y-madwen – Corwen)

**The route.** From Nant-y-madwen continue south-west down the path to Bwlch Coch, at SJ119445, then on to the Grouse Inn at Carrog. (1) From Carrog take the B5437 west towards Corwen, to the junction with the B5436 at SJ105437. Turn right here, taking the B5436 up the hill for a quarter of a mile to SJ105441. Now take the footpath on the left which heads west to the north of Rhagatt Hall until it reaches the B5437 Corwen Road at SJ091438. Continue west along this road, past the ancient British encampment called Caer Drewyn (2) at SJ087444, then one can cross over the Dee bridge into Corwen. (3)

**(1.1) Carrog – the Railway Station.** Like so many rural railways in Britain, the line through the Dee Valley was closed in 1963 by the infamous, short-sighted Doctor Beeching. Fortunately, the line was saved from total extinction by enthusiasts who formed the Llangollen Railway Society. The station at Carrog, and others on this line, have now been painstakingly restored by dedicated members of this society.

**(1.2) Carrog – Glyndwr's Mound.** Just to the south-east of Carrog, is a tree-grown mound which was originally the site of a Norman castle. It was later part of the ancestral home of Owain Glyndwr whose mansion – once the centre-piece of his forty square-mile Glyndyfrdwy estate – stood in the adjacent field. According to tradition, it was on this mound that Owain was formally proclaimed Prince of Wales on 16th September 1400, thus beginning his audacious uprising against Henry IV.

**(2) Caer Drewyn near Corwen.** This is the site of an ancient British encampment. It lies on the summit of the westernmost tip of the Llantysilio Range. Today, unfortunately, the stone ramparts are all that remain visible of the fort. It is supposed to be one of the chain of posts from Dyserth to Cynwyd, and formed in olden times as a stronghold. Owen Gwynedd occupied it in the days of Henry II. (Now open to the public)

**(3) Corwen.** The small market town of Corwen is on the old London–Holyhead coaching road – now the A5. Situated at the foot of the Berwyn mountains, on the banks of the Dee, the population in 1852 stood at 2,199, most of whom were employed in trades connected with agriculture. Here, for many years travellers passing along this road, and the route from Bala to Chester, have halted and refreshed themselves at ancient inns, such as the Royal Oak, Harp, Crown and Owain Glyndwr.

One can imagine the scene in the middle years of the 19th century as the Shrewsbury–Holyhead Mail Coach thundered dramatically into town, and with the horn blowing, and much clattering of hooves, came to a timely halt outside one of these taverns. It was, in fact, also in the Owain Glyndwr Inn where the celebrated foot-traveller, George Henry Borrow, slaked his not inconsiderable thirst. Corwen's other great claim to fame was that the first eisteddfod was held here, way back in the 18th century.

## Section 5. Llangollen – Corwen.
## (5. 3. Nant-y-madwen – Corwen)

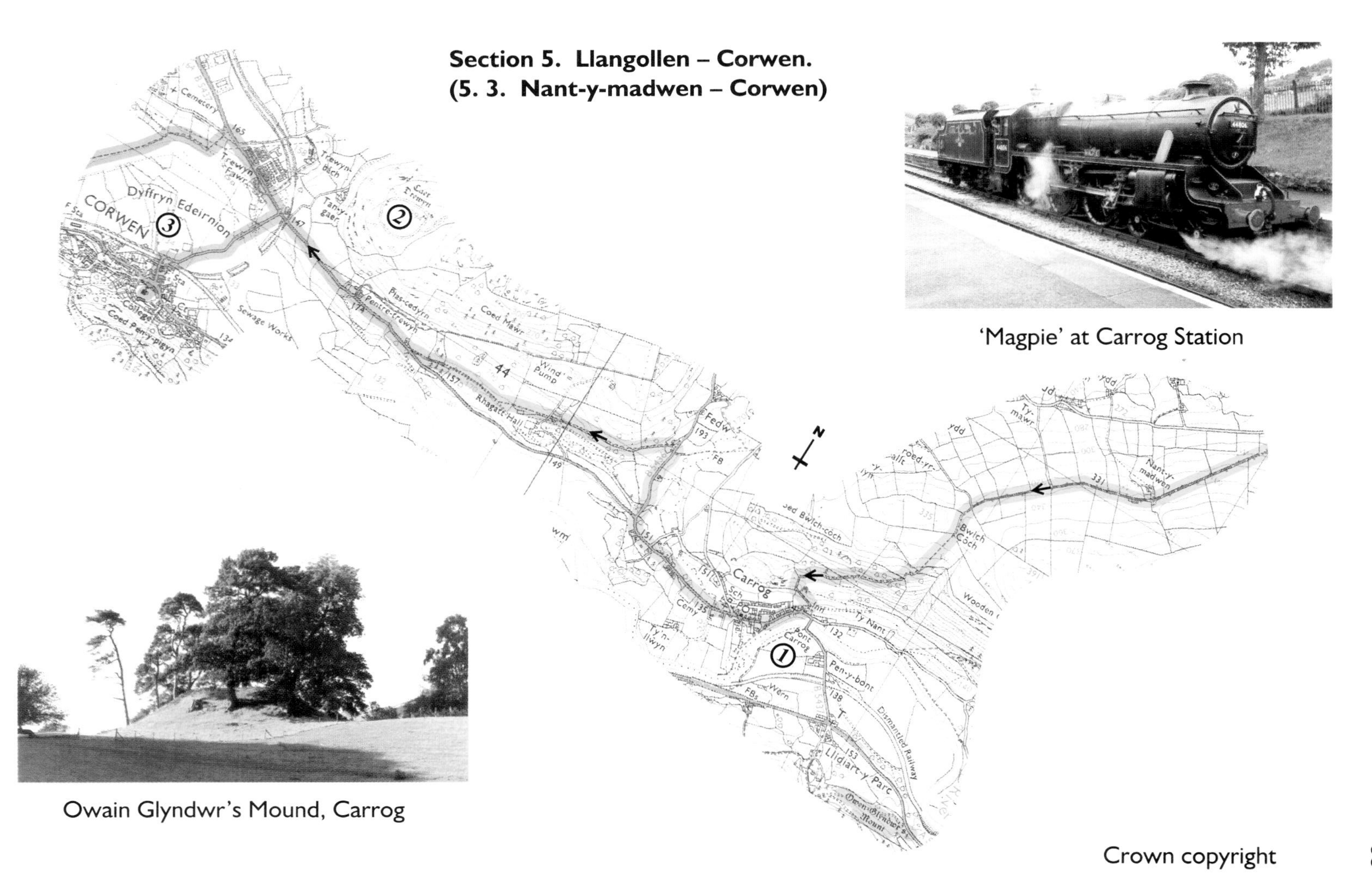


'Magpie' at Carrog Station

Owain Glyndwr's Mound, Carrog

## Section 6. Corwen – Pentre-llyn-cymmer. 15 miles.
## (6.1. Corwen – Betws Gwerfil Goch)

**The route.** From the centre of Corwen, head north back over the Dee bridge to the 'T' Junction. Turn left along the B5437 for a quarter of a mile to SJ078443. Turn left here, taking the footpath along the north-west bank of the Dee to Pont Corwen at SJ069434. (For those who wish to see Rug Chapel (1) turn right at this point and follow the A5 to the first cross-roads, then turn right. The chapel is on the left, a few hundred yards up the A494.) (A shorter alternative to the start of this route is along the main road from the centre of Corwen to Pont Corwen.)

The main route from Pont Corwen crosses over the A5 here and continues to the west past Aber Alwen and on to Cefn Rug on the A5 at SJ054437. Turn left here, then take the lane on the right just before the A5 bridge over the Alwen. Continue along this lane, past the footbridge over the Alwen at Pen-y-Bont, then follow the lane to the right and up to the 'T' Junction at SJ043439. Turn left and continue along the lane to SJ040442, which is just below Ty'n-y-celyn farm. Turn right here, take the footpath up the hill and to the north, past Coed Cadnor and New Covert to the lane at SJ035457. Turn left here and continue north to Betws Gwerfil Goch. (2)

**(1) Rug chapel.** This ancient place of worship is well worth a visit for it is one of the most unusual buildings in North Wales. It was built as a private chapel in 1637 for Colonel William Salusbury – a true-blue Royalist who was shortly destined to enter the pages of history as the stubborn defender of Denbigh Castle against Oliver Cromwell's forces in the Civil War. The chapel's modest exterior gives no indication of the wonderful examples of late medieval craftsmanship within. The roof is elaborately carved and painted from end to end. A truly amazing carved chandelier hangs from the roof, and carvings and paintings also cover the family pews and a gallery. All of which faithfully reflects the Colonel's 'High Church' religious outlook. (The chapel is open May–September 10.00 am–2.00 pm and 3.00 pm–5.00 pm. Closed Sunday and Monday except Bank Holiday weekends.)

**(2) Betws Gwerfil Goch and the Medieval Pilgrims.** The attractive village of Betws Gwerfil Goch (The prayer-house of Gwerfil the Red) lies in a deep valley close to the Afon Alwen. Of particular interest to present-day long-distance walkers is the fact that the village lies on the ancient Pilgrims' Track which once carried the faithful across Wales, from the shrine of St. Winifred at Holywell in the north, to the tomb of St. David in his Pembrokeshire cathedral in the south. In fact, the narrow lane from Betws Gwerfil Goch, heading north-east via Melin-y-Wig and Ffynnon Sarah to Clawdd Newydd, once formed part of this long-distance route. In the centre of the village is the Church of St. Mary, founded in the 12th century, to cater for these pilgrims, by Princess Gwerfil of Meirionydd, the beautiful, red-haired granddaughter of King Owain Gwynedd of North Wales. The interior of this ancient place of worship is remarkable. (A key is available to the church in the village.)

## Section 6. Corwen – Pentre-llyn-cymmer (6.1. Corwen – Betws G. G.)

Pont Corwen

Rug Chapel

Crown copyright

## Section 6. Corwen – Pentre-llyn-cymmer. (6.2. Betws Gwerfil Goch – Llanfihangel Glyn Myfyr)

**The route.** From Betws Gwerfil Goch take the road south-east down towards the A5. Then, just after crossing over the bridge at SJ028464 take the side lane on the right up to a left hand bend at SJ025466. Continue to the west on the path which runs above and to the south of the Afon Alwen to a side lane and bridge over the Alwen at SJ019468. Turn left here, and head due south up the lane beyond Cefn-ceirth to a junction at SJ017466. From this point take the path on the right which heads north-west, then turns south until it rejoins the lane at SJ011471. Turn right here, and continue north-west along the lane past Nant-y-geuryd and a cattle grid to SJ003475. Turn right here, following the path north to Bodtegir at SH005483. From this farm continue to the west on the path which leads to the lane above Llanfihangel at SH998483. Turn right here, and take the lane north-west down the hill to the Crown Inn, by the bridge over the Alwen, at Llanfihangel Glyn Myfyr. (1)

**(1) Owain Myfyr of Llanfihangel Glyn Myfyr.** Owain Myfyr, whose real name was Owen Jones, was born at Llanfihangel Glyn Myfyr in 1749. He became a rich merchant in London, but his interest in life was in history and, in particular, old Welsh manuscripts. His great collection subsequently formed the nucleus of the Myfyrian Archaiology of Wales. He was also responsible for the publication of Dafydd ap Gwilym's poetry. A tablet has been erected in the village to his memory by the Honourable Society of Cymrodorian.

The Church of St. Mary, Betws Gwerfil Goch

## Section 6. Corwen – Pentre-llyn-cymmer
## (6.2. Betws G. G. – Llanfihangel G.M.)

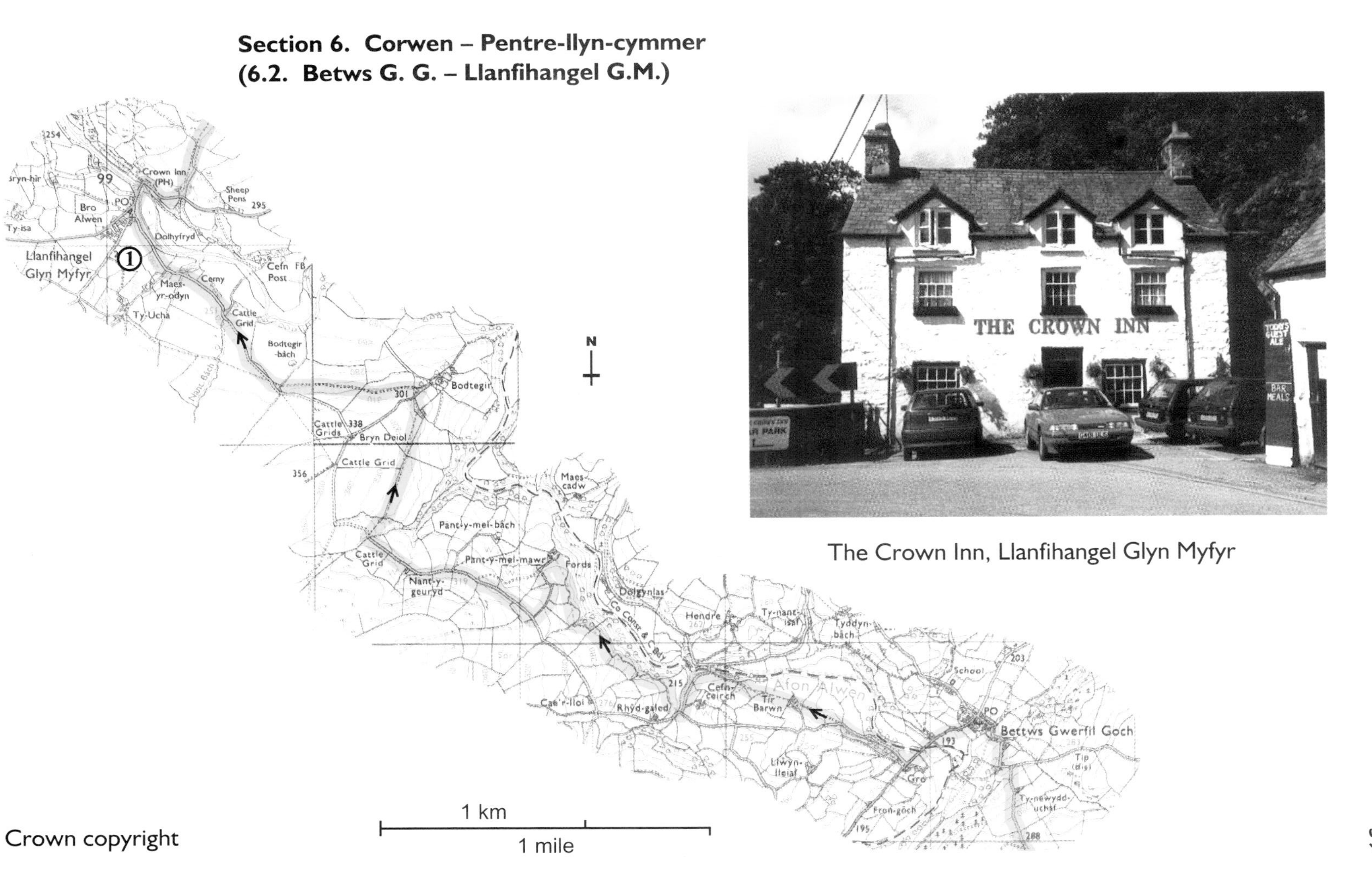


The Crown Inn, Llanfihangel Glyn Myfyr

**Section 6. Corwen – Pentre-llyn-cymmer. (6.3. Llanfihangel Glyn Myfyr – Pentre-llyn-cymmer)**

**The route.** From the Crown Inn at Llanfihangel take the B5105 towards Clawdd-newydd for about a quarter of a mile to SH993492. Now take the footpath on the left which runs up the hill to a lane at Foel. Head north to the sharp bend in the lane at Bryn-y-gwrgi (SH996506). Continue north along the path, forest tracks and a lane to Tal-y-cafn Isaf (SH994520). Now walk down the lane to the Afon Alwen at SH989518. From here take the track on the right, which runs alongside the Afon Alwen to Pentre, which lies just below the Alwen and Brenig Reservoirs. (1)

**(1) The Alwen and Brenig Reservoirs.** In 1907 Birkenhead Corporation was empowered to impound the waters of the Rivers Alwen and Brenig. The first stone of the Alwen Dam was laid in 1911. Work was completed in 1916. The Alwen pipeline then took water to some local users, but most went directly to Cross Hill Reservoir, Birkenhead. Land for the Brenig Reservoir was acquired soon after 1907 by Birkenhead, but the site was not surveyed until 1948. Meanwhile, the Dee and Clwyd River Board Act empowered it to construct the Bala Lake Works to control discharges into the Dee.

Now as a participant in a regional scheme Birkenhead no longer needed to proceed alone with the Brenig reservoir, but work was started in 1973 on the Brenig Dam by the Welsh Water Authority, as part of the Dee Regulation Scheme. Opened in 1976 it took four years to fill. The direct piped supply from Alwen now goes to North-East Wales, whilst the waters of Llyn Brenig, Llyn Celyn and Llyn Tegid (Bala) are now used to regulate the flow of water into the Dee so that water can be abstracted far downstream. In 1992 the abstractions from the Dee were:- North West Water, 709.0 million litres a day, Chester Waterworks Company, 34.1 million litres a day, Wrexham and East Denbighshire Water Company 34.1 million litres a day, Dwr Cymru, Welsh Water (Hyder) 23.6 million litres a day and the British Waterways Board, for the Llangollen canal, 28.4 million litres a day.

The Alwen Dam

## Section 6. Corwen – Pentre-llyn-cymmer.
## (6.3. Llanfihangel G. M. – Pentre-llyn-cymmer)

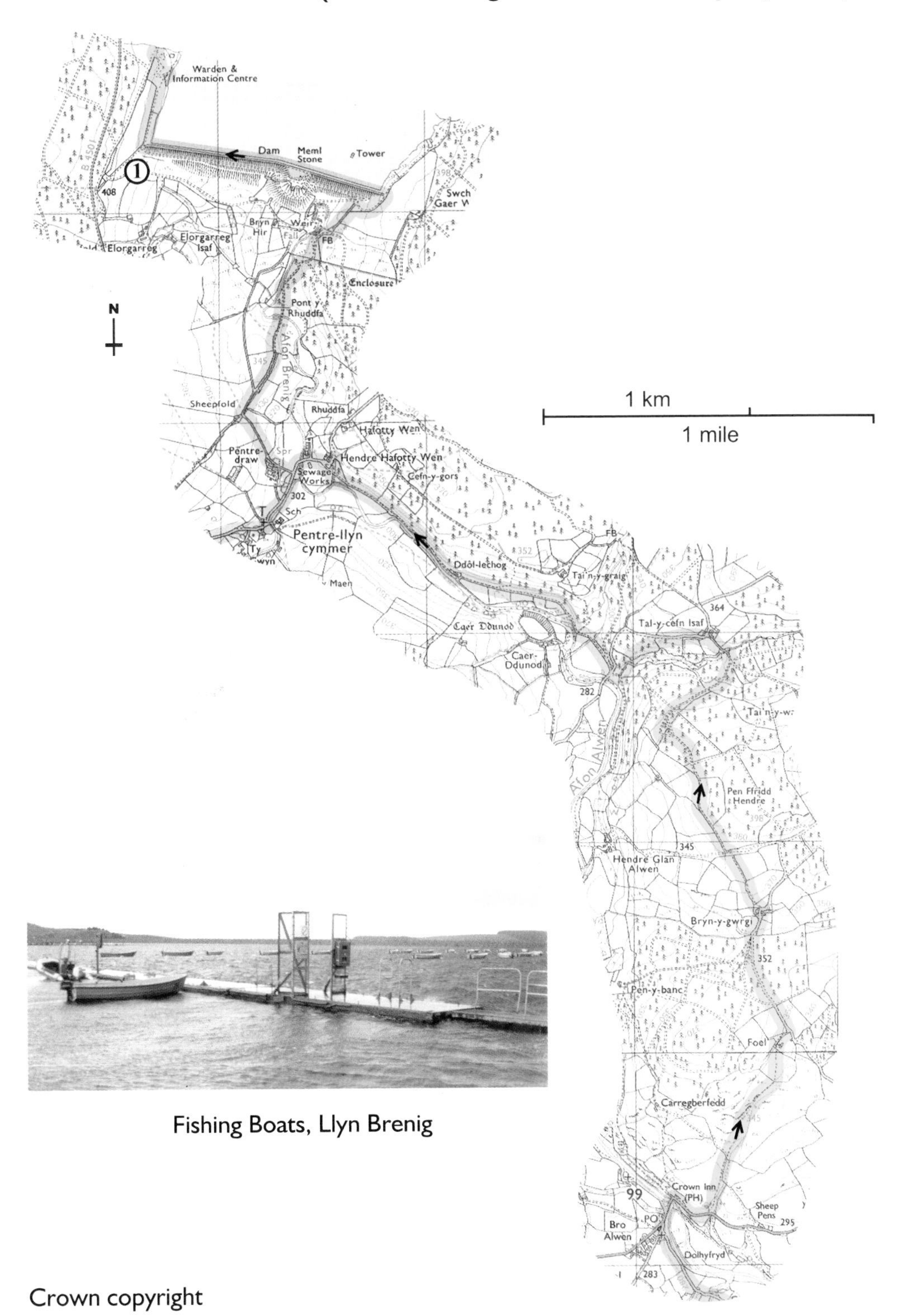


Fishing Boats, Llyn Brenig

## Section 7. Pentre – Cyffylliog. 14 miles. (7.1. Pentre – N.W. Clocaenog)

**The route.** From the road at Pentre-llyn-cymmer (SH973527) take the side lane which heads north-west to SH971530. Turn right here, and right again at the fork in the lane, and continue north over the Afon Brenig bridge at SH973535. Now continue to the eastern end of the Brenig Dam at SH978541. Head west across the dam, and then north, to the Visitor Centre. From here take the well-marked tourist tracks and paths up the west side of Llyn Brenig (1) to the cattle grid at SH966577 on the B4501.

Follow the B4501 north-east, then take the new path which circles round the north end of Brenig to SH983575. From here take the lake-side track to SH986567. Now turn away from the lake and follow the marked Archaeological Trail (2) up the hill to the edge of the Clocaenog forest at SH993564. Move inside the forest fence here then continue north-east on the bridleway through the forest towards Cyffylliog.

**(1) Llyn Brenig.** Llyn Brenig is now a major tourist, sailing and fishing attaction. In 1976 Brenig was stocked with 20,000 trout, and today there are fish rearing cages, where thousands of trout are reared. Trial sailing was also undertaken on Brenig in 1976. A boat park was constructed, and a sailing club formed. At the Visitor Centre today there is a cafe and craft shop. A 10.5 mile walk round the lake with a cycle ride that is slightly longer has been established. The choice of activities now available also includes bird watching, and sub-aqua diving.

**(2) The Archaeological Trail.** Details of an 'Archaeological Trail' round Llyn Brenig are available at the Centre. This is based on a survey made between 1973 and 1975 mainly by the Universities of North Wales and Manchester and related extensive excavation work. Among their 'finds' were a Mesolithic camp site dating back 7,500 years, a series of Bronze Age barrows, a Bronze Age cemetery, and the Hafotai Settlement, dated to about the 16th century. A permanent exhibition at the Centre graphically illustrates these discoveries.

The Visitor Centre, Llyn Brenig

## Section 7. Pentre-llyn-cymmer – Cyffylliog.
## (7.1. Pentre-llyn-cymmer – N.W. Clocaenog)

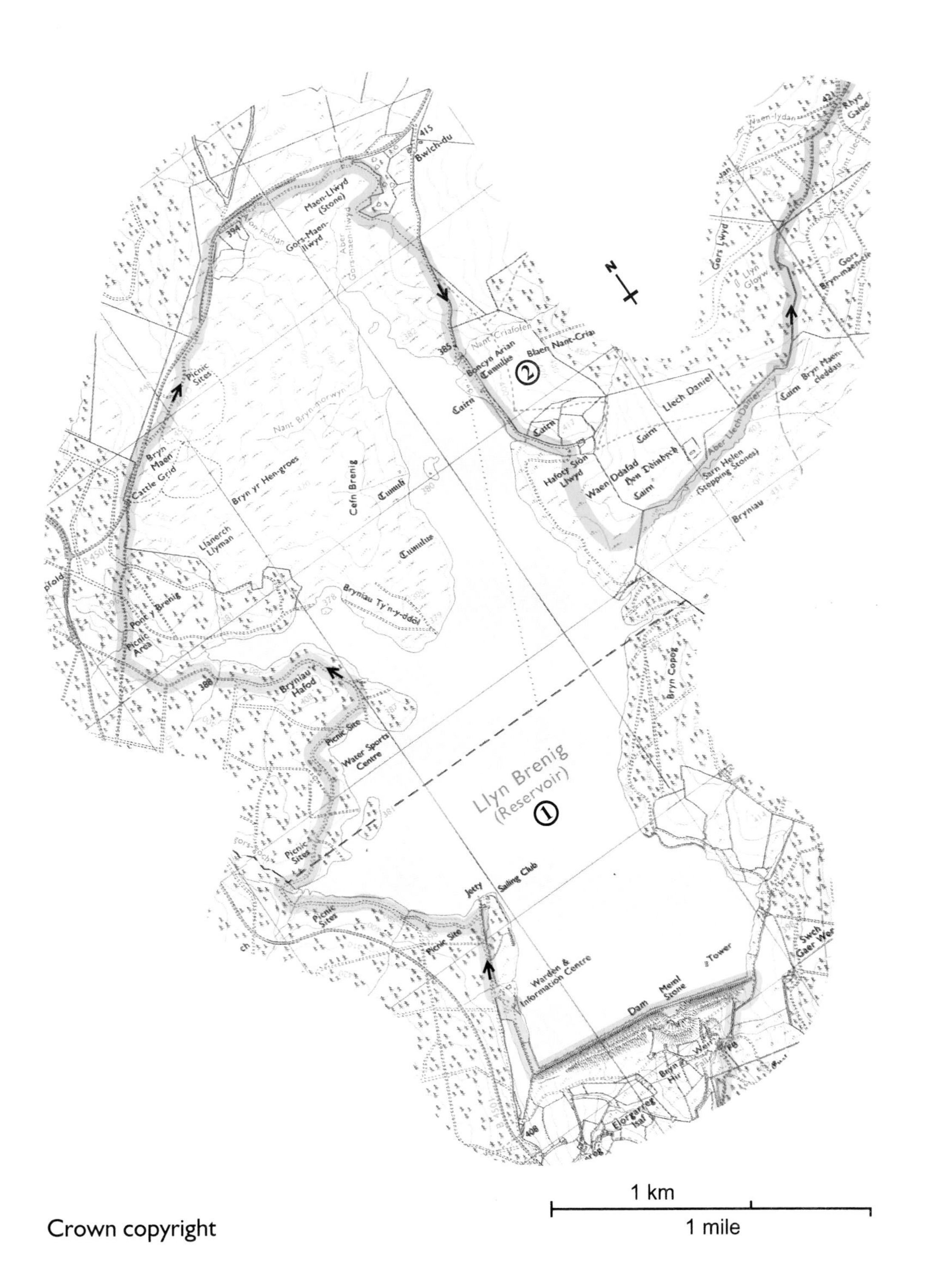

## Section 7. Pentre-llyn-cymmer – Cyffylliog. (7.2. N.W. Clocaenog – Cyffylliog)

**The route.** Continue on the bridleway through the Clocaenog Forest past the junction in the tracks at Rhyd Galed, and on to the Clywedog Reservoir at SJ008574. Here bear left off the main forest track and follow the line of the bridleway running by Bryn Du, which then continues round the south side of Bryn Ocyn and on to the lane at Boced (SJ029583). Now head north-east down the lane to the bridge over the Afon Concwest at SJ035594. Continue to the south-east along the path/track on the north side of the Afon Concwest down to Cyffylliog. (1)

**(1) Cyffylliog.** The small village of Cyffylliog is considered by many to be one of the best places for trout fishing in North Wales. There is also an excellent pub in the village and, as already mentioned, in 1930 one of the first four Youth Hostels to be opened was the one in the Old School at Cyffylliog. The Lord Mayor of Liverpool, Mr Lawrence Holt, himself a keen climber and walker, with Barclay Baron, the Chairman of 'Toc H', were prominent among the prime movers in this progressive venture.

The Chapel, Cyffylliog

## Section 7. Pentre-llyn-cymmer – Cyffylliog.
## (7.2. N. W. Clocaenog – Cyffylliog)

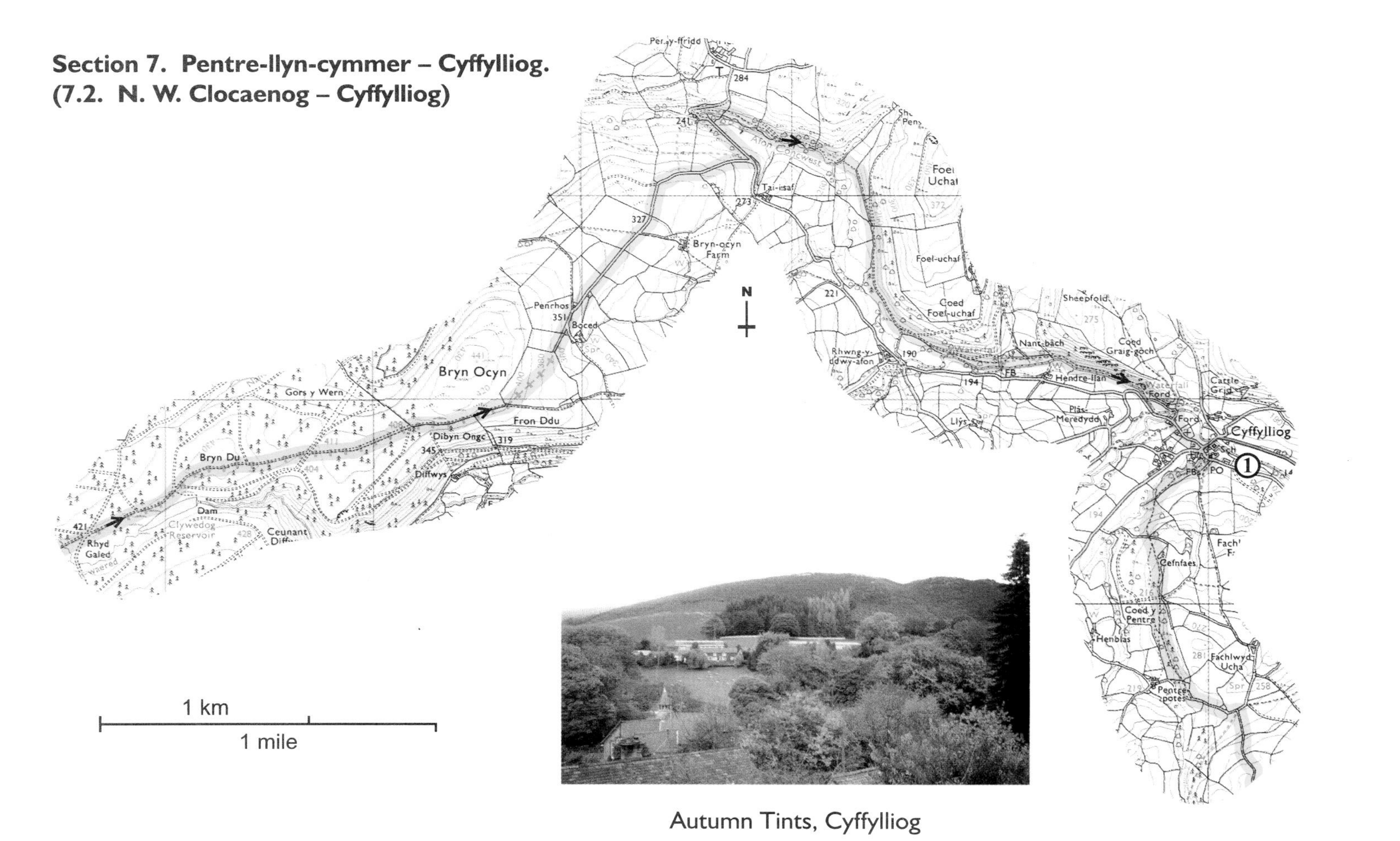


Autumn Tints, Cyffylliog

## Section 8. Cyffylliog – Trefnant. 15 miles. (8.1. Cyffylliog – Rhewl/Ruthin)

**The route.** The route now runs south from Cyffylliog, through the forest, and on to the southern edge of the plantation, near Pentre Potes at SJ059566. Here bear left along a path/track and on to a lane at SJ061565. Now head south-east into the Clocaenog Forest, to the road/footpath junction at SJ065557. (At this point it is well worth making a small diversion along the well-marked tracks to the Bagot Monument (1) at Pincyn Llys at SJ065551.) Otherwise, turn left at the above junction, and follow the lane down the hill towards Bontuchel for about 1 mile, to where the lane bends sharply to the left then, just before Pistyll-gwyn, at SJ081571, take the woodland track on the right which leads down to Bontuchel.

At Bontuchel take the road back towards Cyffylliog, but only to the bridge over the Afon Clywedog. Cross over the bridge, then turn right at the 'T' junction. Now follow the lane for a quarter of a mile to a sharp left-hand bend. Here take the track on the right, known locally as Lady Bagot's Drive, down to Rhewl on the A525 Ruthin–Denbigh road at SJ109604. (To visit the historic town of Ruthin (2) cross the footbridge on the right, off Lady Bagot's Drive, as indicated, at SJ102596.)

**(1) The second Lord Bagot and the Clocaenog Forest.** The Clocaenog Forest, covers much of the highland area west of the Vale of Clwyd. Few who walk the area today, however, are aware that Clocaenog was originally planted well over 170 years ago by Lord Bagot of Pool Park near Ruthin. The plantations he originally established were to replace timber felled during the Napoleonic Wars. They consisted mainly of Norway Spruce, Larch, Oak and Scots Pine. Unfortunately, most of Bagot's earlier plantations were felled during or immediately after the first World War.

After this terrible conflict the vast cleared areas lay unstocked until a large section of the Pool Park Estate was bought by the Forestry Commission in 1930. The hilltop monument of 1830 at Pincyn Llys commemorates the completion of planting by Lord Bagot. A second tablet, added in 1934, reads: "Lord Bagot's plantations were felled during and after the Great War, 1914–18. The Forestry Commission began to plant Clocaenog Forest in 1930. 1934, R.L. Robinson, Chairman". (It is, I think, worth mentioning that part of Clocaenog was a medieval park associated with Ruthin Castle in the late 13th/14th century.)

The Bridge Hotel, Bontuchel

## Section 8. Cyffylliog – Rhewl.
## (8.1. Cyffylliog – Rhewl/Ruthin)

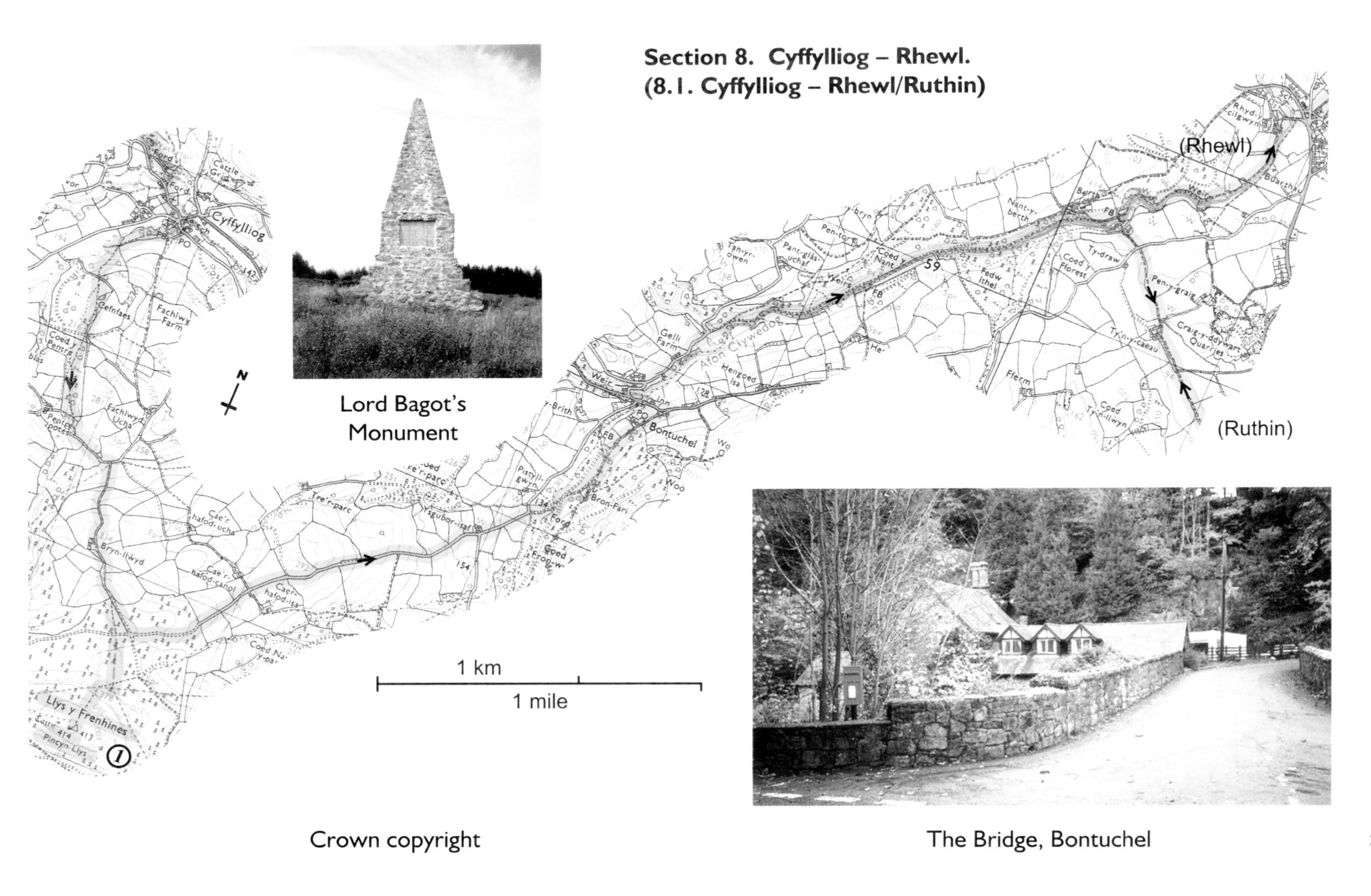

Lord Bagot's Monument

The Bridge, Bontuchel

**(2.1) Ruthin and the 'Marcher' Adventurers.** After the invasion of 1066 adventurers called 'Marchers' moved west into Wales. There was resistance then, in 1267, Prince Llywelyn was formally confirmed by the English as Prince of Wales. Unfortunately, in 1277, Edward I invaded Wales, and drove Llywelyn back into Gwynedd. Edward then commissioned his henchmen to build new castles, granting Denbigh to Henry de Lacy, Earl of Lincoln, and Ruthin to Reginald de Grey. Around these fortresses new fortified towns were founded for English colonisers, many of whom were recruited for this service on the English estates of these lords.

And so it came to pass that in medieval times Welsh inhabitants lived in Well (Welsh) street and Mwrog Street, whereas the English kept close to the castle in Castle Street and Dog Lane, within the line of the 'Pale'. Grey's castle at Ruthin was, of course, the first target of Owain Glyndwr's supporters. The day they chose for the attack was 18th September, 1400, just two days after Owain had assumed the title of Prince of Wales and three days before the town's great annual event, the St. Matthew's Day Fair. They put the town to the torch. Only one building in Well Street and Grey's castle survived.

Ruthin Castle, 1872

**(2.1) Ruthin and the 'Marcher' Adventurers.** After the invasion of 1066 adventurers called 'Marchers' moved west into Wales. There was resistance then, in 1267, Prince Llywelyn was formally confirmed by the English as Prince of Wales. Unfortunately, in 1277, Edward I invaded Wales, and drove Llywelyn back into Gwynedd. Edward then commissioned his henchmen to build new castles, granting Denbigh to Henry de Lacy, Earl of Lincoln, and Ruthin to Reginald de Grey. Around these fortresses new fortified towns were founded for English colonisers, many of whom were recruited for this service on the English estates of these lords.

And so it came to pass that in medieval times Welsh inhabitants lived in Well (Welsh) street and Mwrog Street, whereas the English kept close to the castle in Castle Street and Dog Lane, within the line of the 'Pale'. Grey's castle at Ruthin was, of course, the first target of Owain Glyndwr's supporters. The day they chose for the attack was 18th September, 1400, just two days after Owain had assumed the title of Prince of Wales and three days before the town's great annual event, the St. Matthew's Day Fair. They put the town to the torch. Only one building in Well Street and Grey's castle survived.

**(2.2) Ruthin Castle in later years.** The castle was held for the House of Lancaster during the Wars of the Roses. In the autumn of 1645 Charles I came to Ruthin and the castle was garrisoned for him, to be taken by Colonel Mytton in the April of the following year. Along with other fortresses, Ruthin Castle then became the victim of a Cromwellian demolition order and was finally destroyed in 1648. In 1826, through marriage, the estate and castle passed into the hands of the West family (later Cornwallis-West). The castle had, in fact, become a deplorable ruin when the Hon. Frederick West built on the ground, preserving certain parts of the old fortress, a surprising amount of which is still standing today. Restoration work was begun in 1826, and it was completed in 1852; the end result was the superb castellated mansion which now bears the name Ruthin Castle.

Entrance Gate,
Castell Rhuthun, 1999

## Section 8. Cyffylliog – Trefnant. (8.2. Rhewl – Pont Clawdd-ddu, Denbigh)

The route. From Rhewl take the footpath by the chapel which heads north-east to a lane at SJ114612. Turn right and follow the lane round to the bridge over the River Clwyd at SJ119609. Turn left here, taking the footpath which runs along the east bank of the Clwyd for just under three miles to the lane at Pont Clwyd at SJ099642. Turn right here, then left at the cross roads. Continue north along this lane, past Plas Bennett on your left, and on to the main Denbigh Road by Plas Ffordd Ddwr at SJ099656. (1) Turn left here, and head towards Denbigh (2) for half a mile. At SJ092658, just before the road bridge over the Clwyd, take the footpath on your right which heads north along the east bank of the river to Lleweni Hall.

NB. Those who wish to visit Denbigh should now make a small diversion. From the Clwyd the centre of town is just 2 miles away, which can be reached either by walking along the main road or taking the footpaths as outlined on the strip maps.

**(1) Plas Ffordd-Ddwr.** Of particular interest to climbers is the fact that Andrew Irvine, of 1924 Everest fame, once lived in this impressive house.

**(2) Denbigh Castle.** Dominated by its castle 460 feet above the town, Denbigh has winding streets rich in history, many of which climb up to the Castle, built by the Marcher Lord, Henry de Lacy, Earl of Lincoln, in 1282. The castle as he planned it was a stupendous structure, combining the ornamentation of a baronial hall and the strength of a warlike fortress. Understandably, its builder anticipated the troubles of attacks and sieges, and built accordingly.

In the course of time the castle was granted to Queen Elizabeth's favourite, Robert Dudley, Earl of Leicester. In 1645 King Charles I stayed at the castle after his retreat from Chester, but the following year it was besieged by the Parliamentarians, being the last Welsh castle to hold out for the king. Finally, the garrison was starved into surrender by Cromwell's forces and the castle was largely dismantled. After the restoration of Charles II most of what remained was blown up with gunpowder.

## Section 8. Cyffylliog – Trefnant.
## (8.2. Rhewl – Pont Clawdd-ddu, Denbigh)

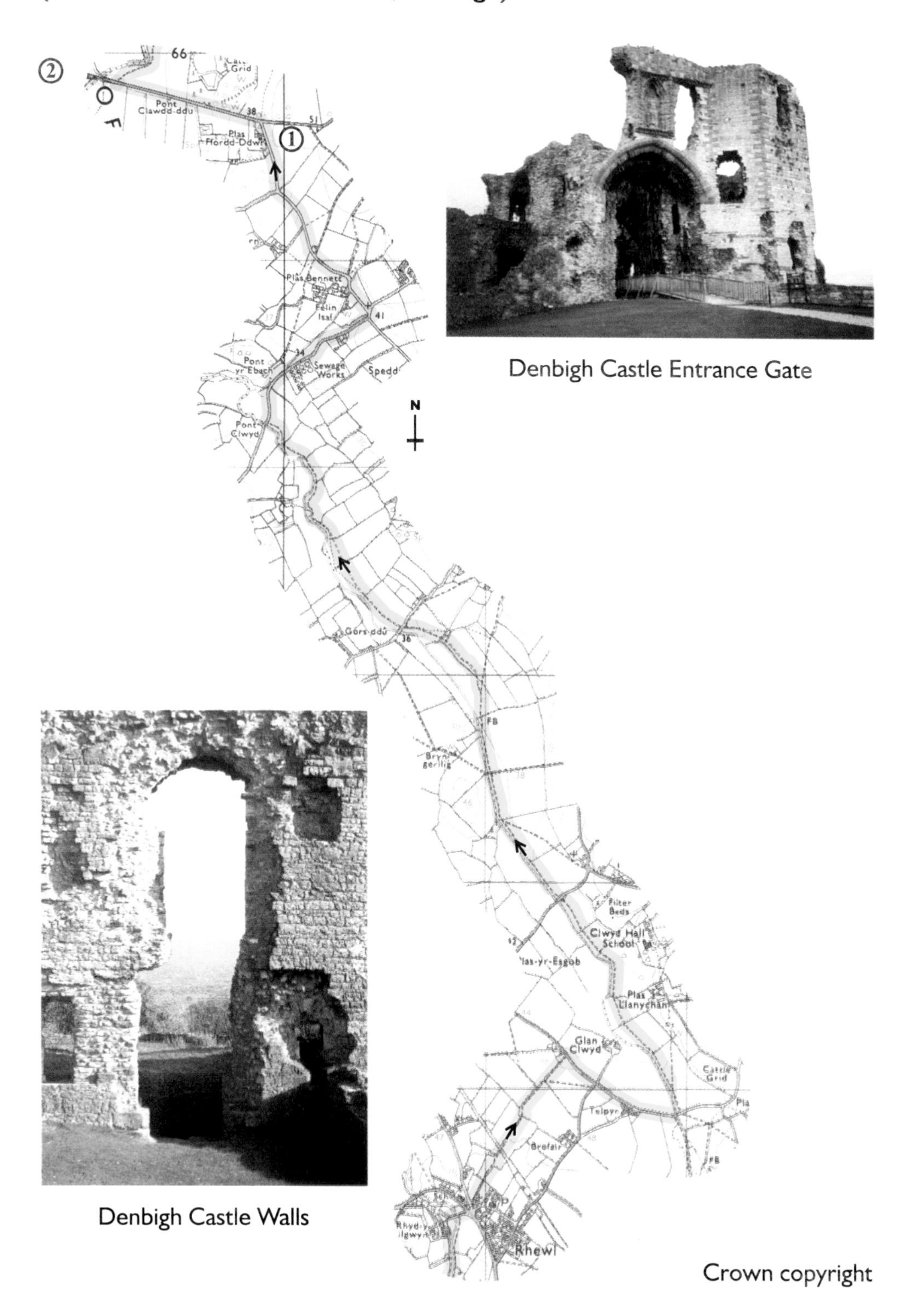


Denbigh Castle Entrance Gate

Denbigh Castle Walls

## Section 8. Cyffylliog – Trefnant. (8.3. Pont Clawdd-ddu – Trefnant)

**The route.** From the Denbigh road, near Denbigh, (1) at SJ092658, take the path along the east bank of the Clwyd to the cattle grid by Lleweni Hall at SJ082687. (2) Turn left here to visit the Hall, otherwise turn right, taking the drive across the meadow land to SJ086690. Turn left here, heading north-west to the A541 at SJ080696 by Pontruffydd Hall Farm. Turn left now and continue round the bend on the A541 towards the Trefnant/Tremeirchion cross-roads at SJ066701. Turn right and continue north-east towards Tremeirchion for a quarter of a mile to Dedwyddfa Farm at SJ068704.

**(1) Denbigh as it was in 1852.** "There are places of worship [in Denbigh] for Baptists, Independents, Calvinists, and Wesleyan Methodists. The town also contains a free grammar-school for twenty boys; a blue-coat charity-school, on the foundations of which are twenty-four boys; and a national school, in which eighty-six boys and one hundred girls are educated. Denbigh has a good town-hall, an excellent market-house, a new assembly-room, a dispensary, a reading-room, and a Welsh literary society. Its chief manufactures are gloves and shoes; the market is held on a Wednesday and Saturday. There is also a branch of the North and South Wales Bank here." (From John Hicklin''s Illustrated Handbook of North Wales, Chester, 1852.)

**(2) Lleweni Hall.** The history of Lleweni goes back a very long way. According to tradition it all began in 720 AD when Machweithiau, Chief of one of the fifteen Noble Tribes of Wales settled here. The place was later occupied by Prince David, Lord of Denbigh and brother of Prince Llewelyn ap Gruffydd; then the hall became the seat of the Salusburys. Sir John Salusbury of Lleweni was constable of Denbigh Castle in 1530. He died in 1578. His son, John Salusbury Esq., was the member of this house who had the dubious distinction of marrying 'Catherine Tudor of Berain'.

Catherine was the granddaughter of an illegitimate son of Henry VII by a Breton woman he met while he was in exile. After Salusbury died Catherine had three further marriages. Legends then grew up that she had had six husbands in all, and as she tired of them she killed them successively by pouring molten lead in their ears as they slept! Her last husband, assuming that he was next in line for this robust ear treatment, is supposed to have locked her up in a room and starved her to death! She died in 1591 and was buried at Llanyffyd. Not surprisingly, perhaps, there is no memorial to her.

Lleweni was bought by the Rev. Edward Hughes of Kinmel in 1810, then, just six years later, it was almost entirely demolished by his son, the future Lord Dinorben. The large, semi-derelict building near the hall were once stables. Today, Lleweni Hall, in the heart of the Vale of Clwyd, is a delightful 'Bed & Breakfast' establishment. (Visitors can be shown around the hall by prior arrangement.)

## Section 8. Cyffylliog – Trefnant. (8.3. Pont Clawdd-ddu – Trefnant)

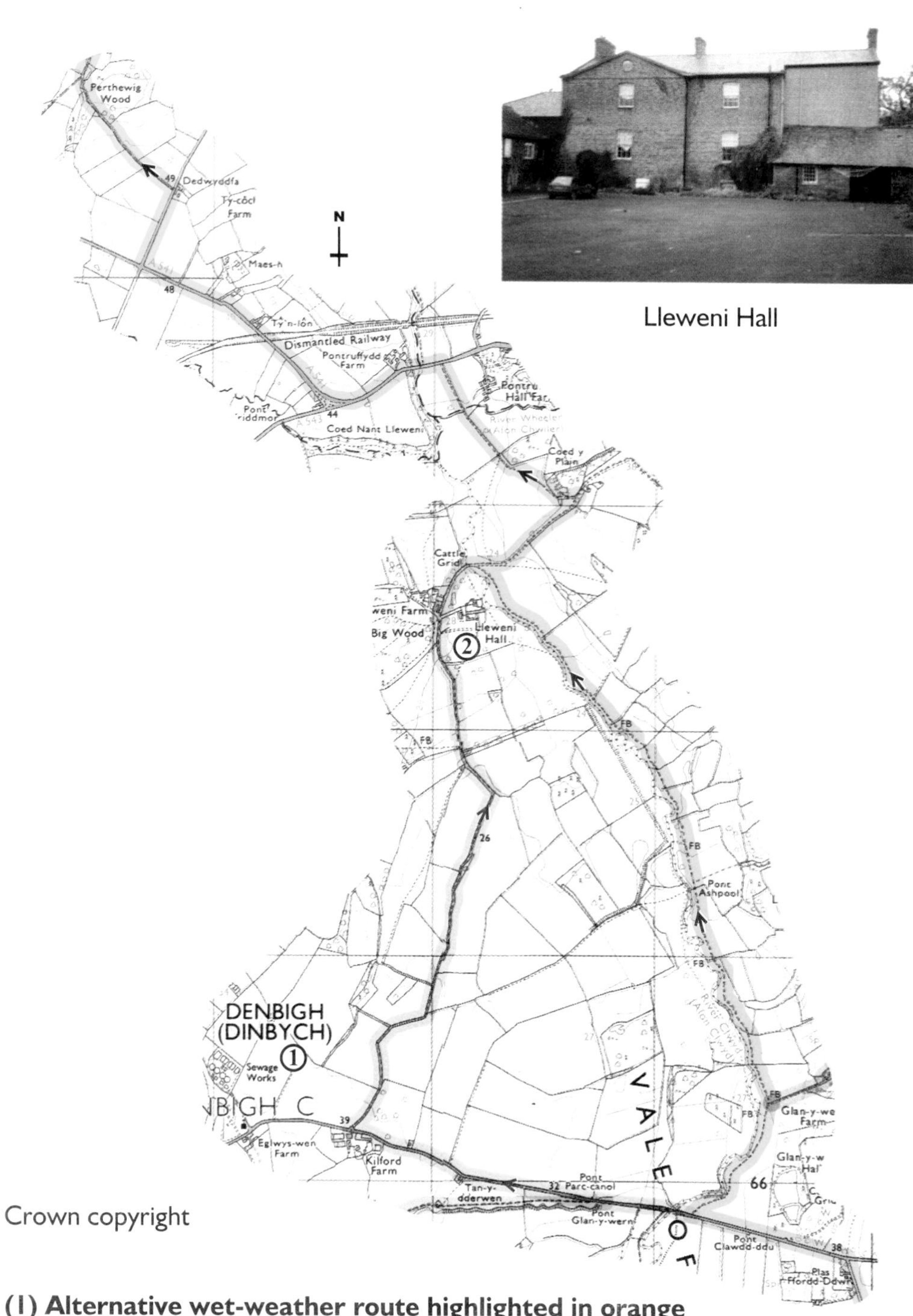


Lleweni Hall



**(1) Alternative wet-weather route highlighted in orange**
**(2) West end of link path highlighted in blue**
**(3) North end of Llansannan alternative route highlighted in purple**

## Section 9. Trefnant – Prestatyn. 17 miles. (9.1 Trefnant – St. Asaph)

**The route.** From Dedwyddfa Farm head north-west on the bridleway through Perthewig Wood, to Pethewig Farm at SJ064710. From here continue on to the lane by Dolbelidr at SJ057716. Turn right here and head up the lane towards Tremeirchion for a quarter of a mile. Take the path on the left here which leads to the southern edge of Dormitory Wood at SJ061727, by the road. Now turn left and continue north-west along the footpaths which lead directly into St. Asaph. (1) At the cross roads by the Cathedral head north-east down Chester Street to the bridge over the Expressway at Pont Dafydd (SJ045749).

**(1) St. Asaph (Llanelwy).** According to some, but not all historians, the hill on which St. Asaph stands has the ancient name of Bryn Paulin (now Bryn Polyn) from having been made a place of encampment by the Roman Governor, Suetoneus Paulinas, on his way to conquer Anglesey in A.D. 60. Originally, and still called Llanelwy, it owes its establishment to St. Kentigern of Glasgow who, during the middle years of the 6th century, was driven from the north by persecution and took refuge here. No less than 960 monks once gathered round this charismatic figure. On the death of the Prince who had expelled Kentigern from Scotland, his successor, Roderic, recalled that prelate to his duties in the north. Kentigern then consigned the monastery to a local man, Asaph, or Hassaph, by which name it has since been known.

After the Conquest this community was virtually destroyed in the bitter conflicts between the Normans and the local chiefs. The first cathedral, which was made of wood, was burned to the ground in 1282, and being re-erected was once again almost totally destroyed in 1402 by Owain Glyndwr. During the Civil Wars St. Asaph suffered once more, when the cathedral was desecrated. Among other things the font was used as a trough for watering horses, and the episcopal palace converted into a tavern! After this rude occurrence repairs were carried out by Bishop Griffiths (1660-9) and his successor. (The Cathedral is usually open 7.30 a.m.–6.00 p.m; 4.30 p.m. in winter.)

## Section 9. Trefnant – Prestatyn. (9.1. Trefnant – St. Asaph)

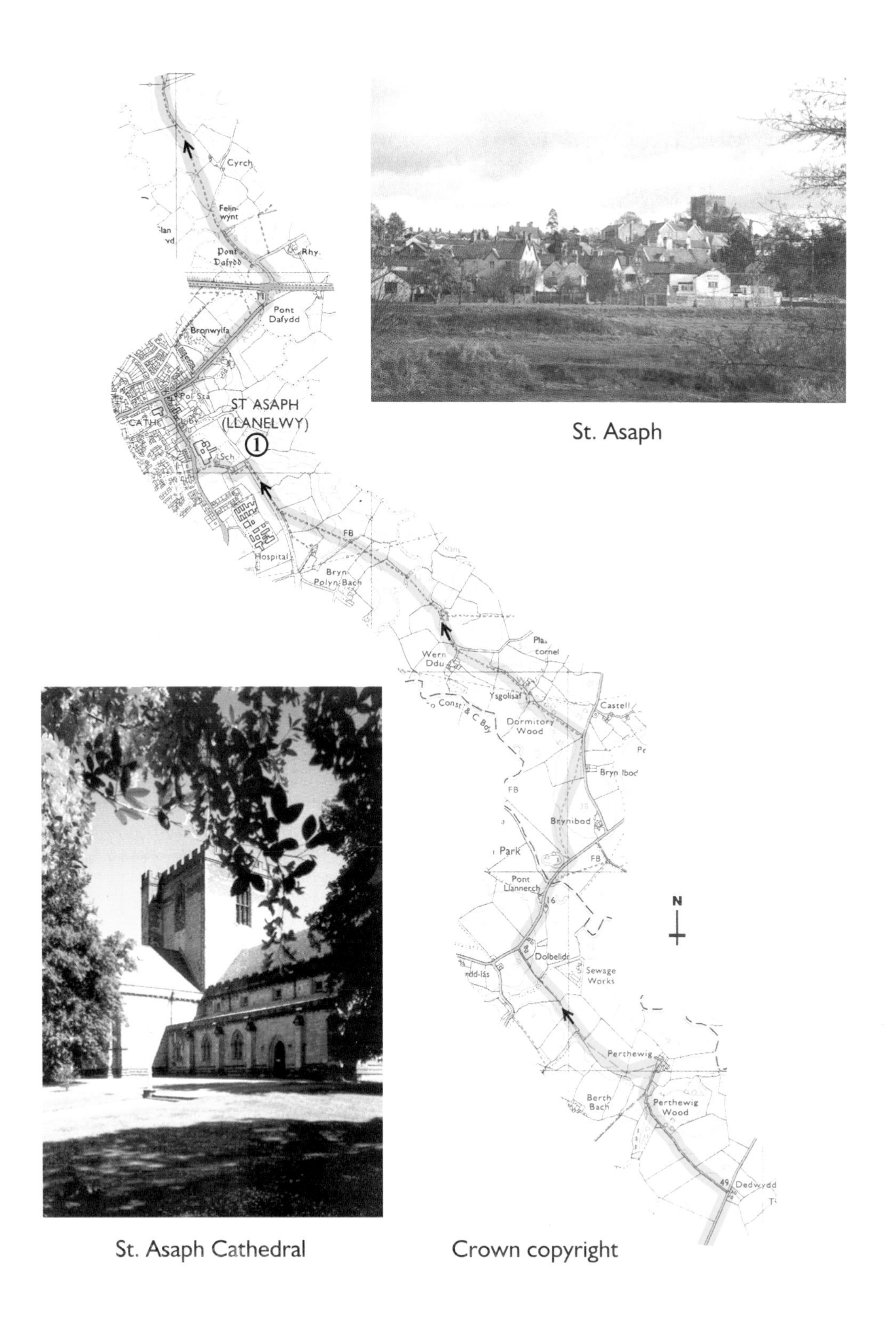


St. Asaph

St. Asaph Cathedral

Crown copyright

**Section 9. Trefnant – Prestatyn. (9.2. St. Asaph – Dyserth)**

**The route.** From the footbridge over the A55 Expressway at Pont Dafydd (SJ045749) continue north along the east bank of the Clwyd to SJ038763. Turn to the east now, taking the path to Ddwylig Isaf on the B5429 at SJ046764. Now turn left, then after 50 yards go through the gate on the right, bear left across the field then follow the path close to the rugby ground, then continue on to the next lane. Turn right and follow the lane past the wood, then take the path on the left that continues directly ahead to the next lane. Continue straight ahead to Tan-y-bryn at SJ064769. Turn right, then sharp left, following the lane round to the next footpath on the left at SJ067771. Head north on this path. At the lane turn left, and make for the church in Cwm at SJ066774.

From the church take the footpath north through Church Wood, across a lane, and on until it reaches the Offa's Dyke Path at SJ068782. From here follow the ODP to Pandy Mill at SJ071792. From the mill take the path along the old rail track to SJ0644793 on the A5151 at Dyserth. (1) Turn left here, cross the main road, then pick up the path marked 'North Wales Path' which runs along the old rail track towards Prestatyn.

**(1) Dyserth.** Dyserth is famous for its remarkable Waterfall which attracts thousands of tourists every year. The town also has a very beautiful church, St. Bridget and St. Cwyfan, which is named after the Welsh saint Cwyfan and the Irish saint Bridget, most highly honoured of Celtic female saints. The building has a bellcote, window and doorway designed by the celebrated Victorian architect, Sir Gilbert Scott, as part of a restoration programme he was responsible for c1873–1875.

Many years ago Dyserth had a great castle. What little is left of this once imposing structure is marked on the map at SJ064799. About 1900 quarrying destroyed most of what remained, but some of the bank and ditch defences can still be seen. Built by the English in 1241 to replace or reinforce their fortress at Rhuddlan, like all the fortresses in North Wales it has been conquered and re-conquered on numerous occasions. Most notably, it was besieged and taken in five weeks in 1263 by Llewellyn the Last of Gwynedd. It was during this siege that it was undermined, razed to the ground, and Einion, the young son of Rhirid the Wolf was slain.

## Section 9. Trefnant – Prestatyn. (9.2. St. Asaph – Dyserth)

Dyserth Waterfall

**Section 9. Trefnant – Prestatyn. (9.3. Dyserth – Prestatyn)**

**The route.** Follow the old rail track out of Dyserth to a point south of Graig Fawr at SJ058802. Here follow the lane up the hill for a few hundred yards to a stile on the left, which leads directly in to the National Trust land of Graig Fawr, and the remarkable viewpoint on the summit. Exit the Trust land at SJ063802. Turn left here, head up the hill, turn left again, then pick up the ODP at SJ065803. Continue on the ODP above Coed yr Esgob to SJ070813. Turn right here, taking the path past King Charles' Bowling Green, Bryn Llwyn (1) (marked Tumulus on the OS map at SJ072814) and on down to Gwaenysgor.* At the road turn right, then first left. Follow this lane to the next footpath on the left at SJ081817, which leads back to your starting point at Prestatyn.

* Those who wish to visit the village should go over the stile on the right by the old well then, from the boardwalk, take the path left into the village.

**(1) King Charles' Bowling Green.** The romantically named King Charles' Bowling Green is one of several rounded summits in this area. Some evidence of Neolithic occupation has certainly been established on the eastward slopes here, and excavations carried out in 1913 tended to confirm this dating. Further archeological work on this site, however, then cast doubt on the 1913 conclusions, for a more objective analysis of all discoveries clearly indicated that they belong to a much later period.

**(2) The Old Well, Gwaenysgor.** The well was the main water supply for the village until the mid 1960's when Gwaenysgor was linked into the Holywell Rural District Council''s supply system. The well was still used until the 1970's because the new supply was not consistent and would fail at times of drought and low pressure. (The village now gets its supply from Llyn Alwen.) The well itself has been restored by the Gwaenysgor Conservation Group but the water is not fit to drink. The low seat structure was probably used to rest the buckets.

The Eagle and Child

## Section 9. Trefnant – Prestatyn. (9.3. Dyserth – Prestatyn)

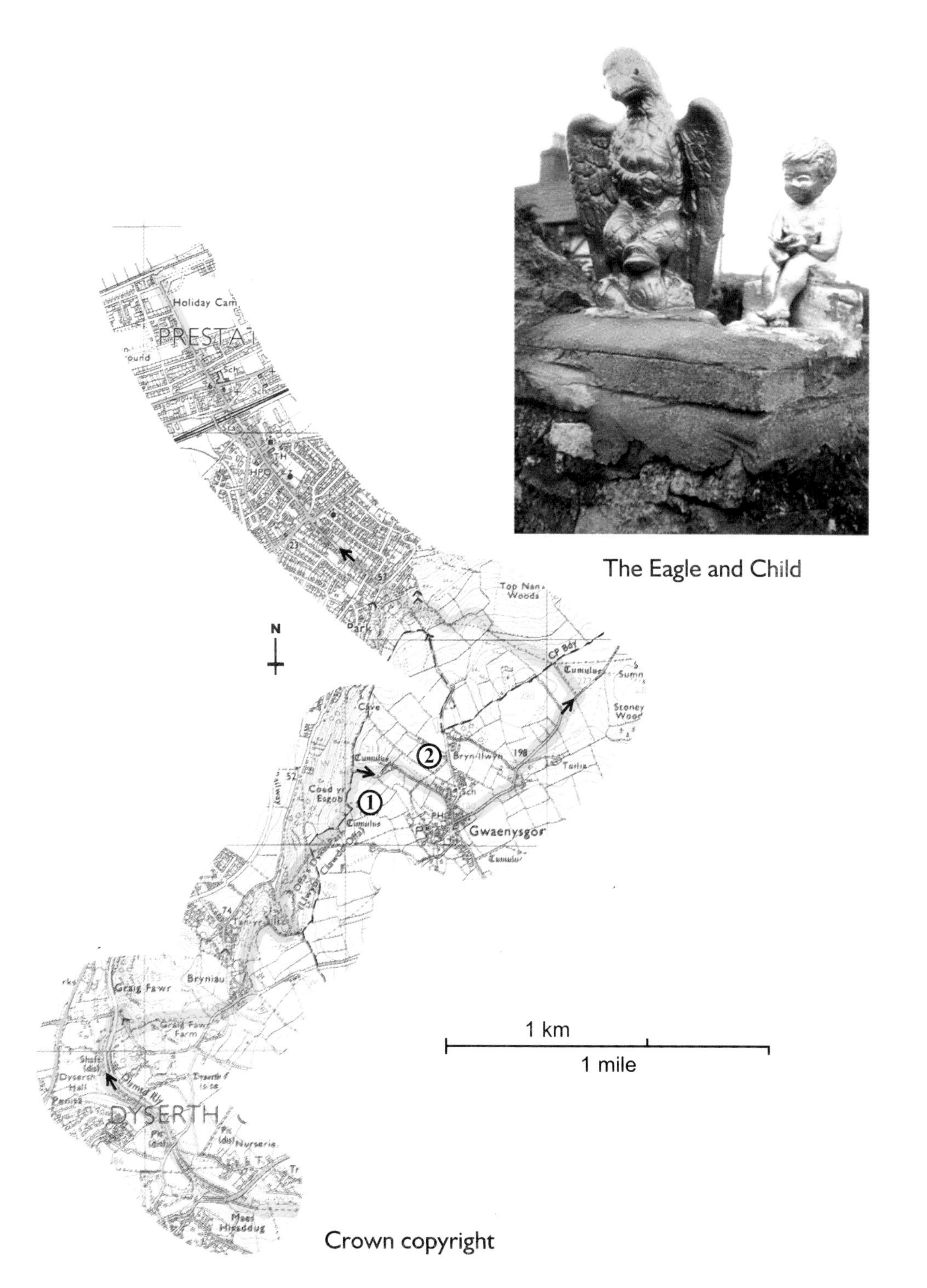


The Eagle and Child

## Section 10. The Llansannan Alternative Route. 30 miles.
## (10.1. Pentre-llyn-cymmer – Pont y Clogwyn)

**The route.** From Pentre-llyn-cymmer take the lane that runs south-east to the B4501, then the track which leads to the Alwen Dam. (1) After viewing the dam return to the main road, turn left then just before the Brenig Dam, take the slip-road on the right which leads to the Brenig Visitor Centre. From here continue north along the west bank of Brenig, past Bryniau'r Hafon, and on to the junction with a long bridleway at SH961571. Turn left here, cross over the B4501 then, after 1.5 miles, take the path on the right which runs north, past Tan-y-graig and Ty Isaf and on to the A543, at Pont y Clogwyn, at SH931569, which is just to the south-east of Llyn Aled.

**(1) The Alwen Reservoir and the Water Industry today.** On 3rd October, 1911, the first stone of the Alwen dam was laid by Alderman Henry Bloor, Chairman of the Birkenhead Water Committee, who opened the Works on 15th August, 1921. The dam is 90 feet high and 458 feet long. The reservoir covers an area of 368 acres. It is about three miles long and half a mile wide. The total capacity of the reservoir is 3,200 million gallons. The surrounding drainage area is 6,313 acres in extent.

In 1989 North West Water was formed and the management of Alwen passed to Welsh Water (Hyder Utilities). The Alwen aqueduct now only supplies water as far as Deeside. North West Water currently supplies 7 million customers in the north-west, including Greater Manchester and Merseyside as well as most of Cheshire, Lancashire and Cumbria. Merseyside, the Wirral and West Lancashire are now primarily supplied by Lake Vyrnwy, the River Dee and the Rivington Reservoirs. In total, this huge undertaking now manages 39 reservoirs, from Haweswater in the north to Vyrnwy (Llyn Efyrnwy) in the south, 4 natural lakes, and abstracts water from 7 rivers (notably the Dee) and 5 groundwater sources. (On the 19th April 2000, Hyder accepted a £402m takeover bid from the Nomura International Bank of Japan.)

The Alwen Dam

## Section 10. Llansannan Alternative Route.
## (10.1. Pentre-llyn-cymmer – Pont y Clogwen)

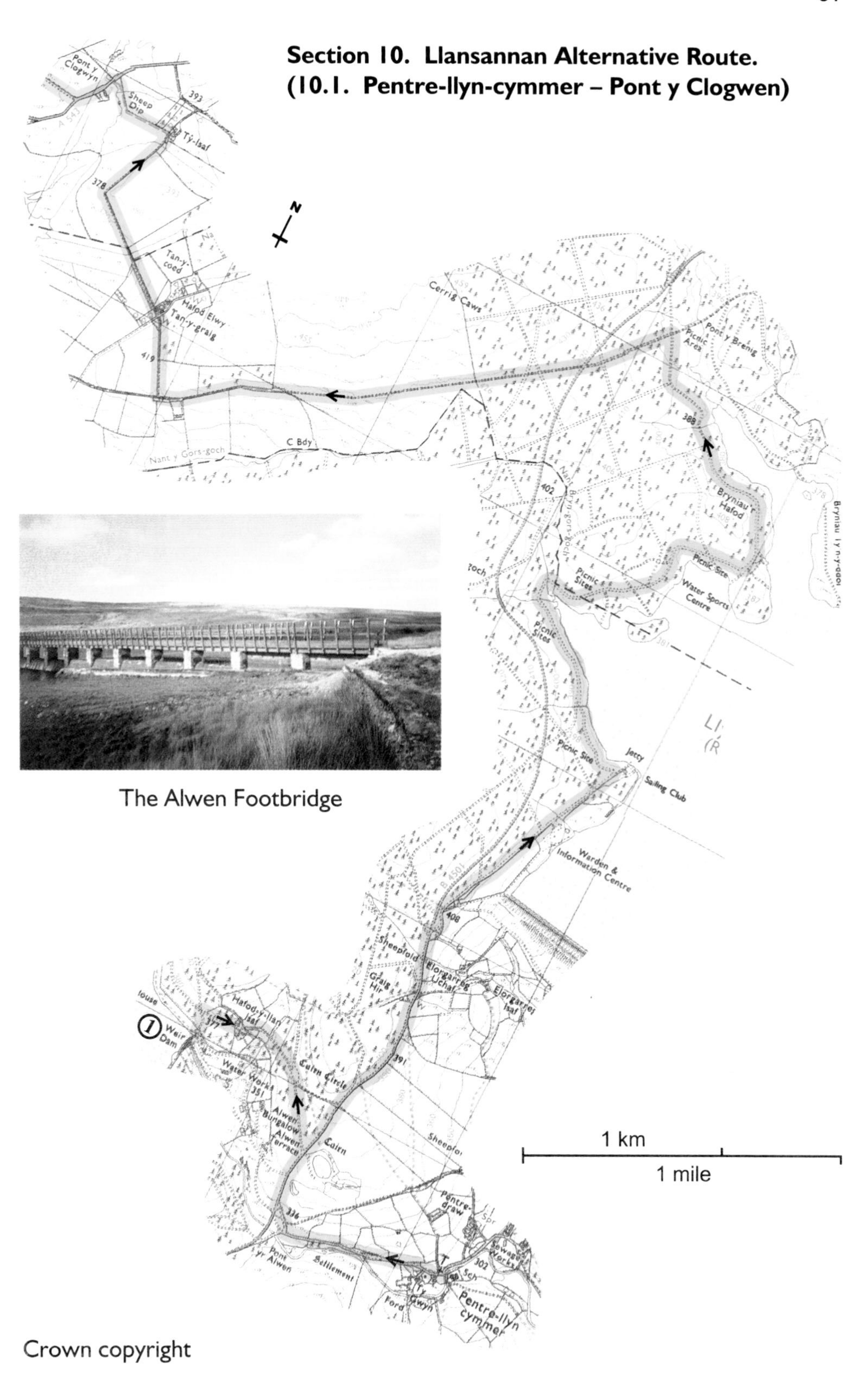


The Alwen Footbridge

**Section 10. The Llansannan Alternative Route.**
**(10.2. Pont y Clogwyn – Cleiriach)**

**The route.** Those who wish to visit the famous Sportsman''s Arms, at SH952590, or view the ruins of Gwylfa Hiraethog (1) near this pub, should now make a short, 2 mile diversion, eastbound, along the A543. Otherwise, from the A543 near Pont y Clogwyn (SH929568) take the secondary moorland road across Mynydd Hiraethog, (2) passing along the east banks of Llyn Aled and Aled Isaf. (3) After crossing over the Aled Isaf Dam, at SH914600, turn sharp right, and follow the path which runs north-east, along the Aled Valley. At Nant-y-Merddyn-Uchaf (SH920612) bear left and follow the new line of the path through the farmyard and then continue north-east to Cleiriach at SH925621.

**(1) Gwylfa Hiraethog – The Watch Tower of Mynydd Hiraethog.** High up on these bleak moorlands, at 1,627 feet, are the sombre ruins of Gwylfa Hiraethog, which in Welsh means the Watch Tower of Mynydd Hiraethog. (1) It was built in 1913 as a shooting lodge for the Merseyside tycoon, Hudson Ewbanke Kearley, first Viscount Devonport (1856–1934), one-time senior partner in the firm of Kearley & Tongue, founder of International Stores, Liberal M.P. for Devonport (1892–1910), and first Chairman of the Port of London Authority.

In part stone-built, a section was also made of wood. The latter part was built in Norway, taken to pieces, and then re-erected in Wales. Writing in 1968 the then Lord Devonport stated that the family's annual visit to the lodge always caused great excitement. The long journey from Denbigh, he recalled, would be made by horse-drawn wagonette, and every day during the shooting season a dogcart would be sent down to Denbigh, to fetch provisions. In 1925 Lord Devonport sold the Lodge. It was never again inhabited. However, because of its isolated and dramatic appearance since being vacated it has appeared in many TV productions including Wuthering Heights.

**(2) Mynydd Hiraethog SSSI.** Mynydd Hiraethog represents one of the four remaining extensive tracts of sub-montane heather, Calluna vulgaris heath in the area. Other ericaceous shrubs of note on the heath are crowberry, Empetrum nigrum, and cowberry, Vaccinium votis-idaea. Dunlin, snipe, curlew, lapwing, common sandpiper, and red grouse, also breed on this moor. Hunting and nesting raptors include peregrine falcon, kestrel, buzzard, merlin, hen harrier and short-eared owl. A large colony of black-headed gulls is also present.

**(3) Llyn Aled and Aled Isaf Reservoirs.** The Llyn Aled dam was completed in 1934. This increased the level of the existing Llyn Aled. The Aled Isaf dam was completed in 1938. Both reservoirs are linked and control the flow of water into the Afon Aled. These impounding reservoirs were originally intended to supply water directly to Rhyl and Prestatyn, but due to lack of funds the aqueduct was never built. So, by default, the scheme became one of the first river regulating systems.

## Section 10. The Llansannan Alternative Route.
## (10.2. Pont y Clogwyn – Cleiriach)

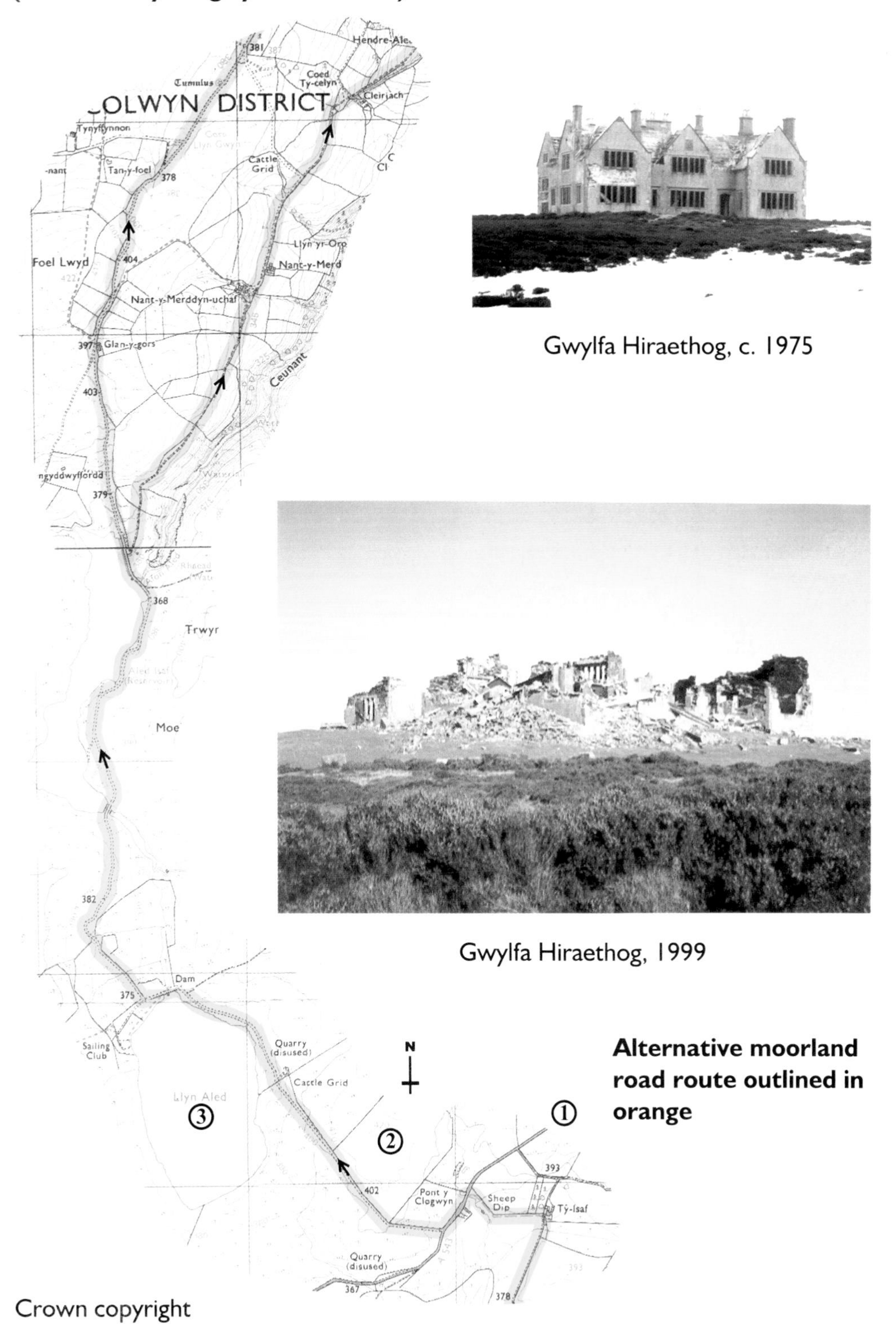


Gwylfa Hiraethog, c. 1975

Gwylfa Hiraethog, 1999

**Alternative moorland road route outlined in orange**

## Section 10. The Llansannan Alternative Route.
## (10.3. Cleiriach – Bryn-Rhyd-yr-Arian)

**The route.** From Cleiriach at SH925621 continue to the north-east, past Hendre Aled and Hendre Aled Cottage, and on to Cae-du at SH932632. After passing through two gates, just below the farm, continue down the hillside, making for the footbridge over the Afon Aled at SH934634. After crossing over the bridge bear left, then right, cross over the fence and follow the path up the north bank of the stream, through the farm-yard, and on to the lane at Rhyd-loew at SH937634.

Turn left at Rhyd-loew, and continue north along the lane to the first junction at Acrau-Isaf. Turn left again, and follow the lane down to Pont Melin-Gadeg (SH936641). The path now continues north along the east bank of the Afon Aled to the bridge at Pont y Nant. Cross over the lane, then continue north, through the woods, and on to the road just south of Llansannan, at Gogal Ganol. Turn right then, after a few hundred yards, take the path on the right which follows the banks of the Afon Aled into Llansannan. (1) Leave Llansannan by the path which runs north-east, firstly along the south, then the north bank of the Afon Aled, and on to the small community of Bryn Rhyd-yr-Arian at SH956673.

**(1) Llansannan.** Llansannan is a small community about 8 miles from Abergele, 9 from Denbigh, and 12 from Llanrwst. The village church – St. Sannan, was originally built in 1777–1778, then modernised in 1879. In 1871 the population of this parish stood at 1,111. At this time, long before the arrival of supermarkets and motor cars, it is interesting to note, the village had two blacksmiths, two boot and shoe makers, a butcher, and a draper – Robert Vaughan.

The famous Llansannan Monument, erected in 1899, portrays a small girl in a Welsh dress, holding a garland of flowers, seated in front of an obelisk. Designed by Gascombe John, it was raised to pay tribute to five writers born in the community. Tudor Aled (c1470–1526), William Salesbury (a translator of the New Testament into Welsh c1520?–1584), Henry Rees (1798–1869), William Rees ('Gwilym Hiraethog', 1802–83), and Iorwerth Glanaled (1819–67). Also in the centre of this remarkable village is another notable monument, the War Memorial, which pays tribute to the disproportionately high number of men from this small rural community who died whilst serving in the Armed Forces in the 1st and 2nd World Wars.

**Section 10. The Llansannan Alternative Route.**
**(10.3. Cleiriach – Bryn-Rhyd-yr-Arian)**

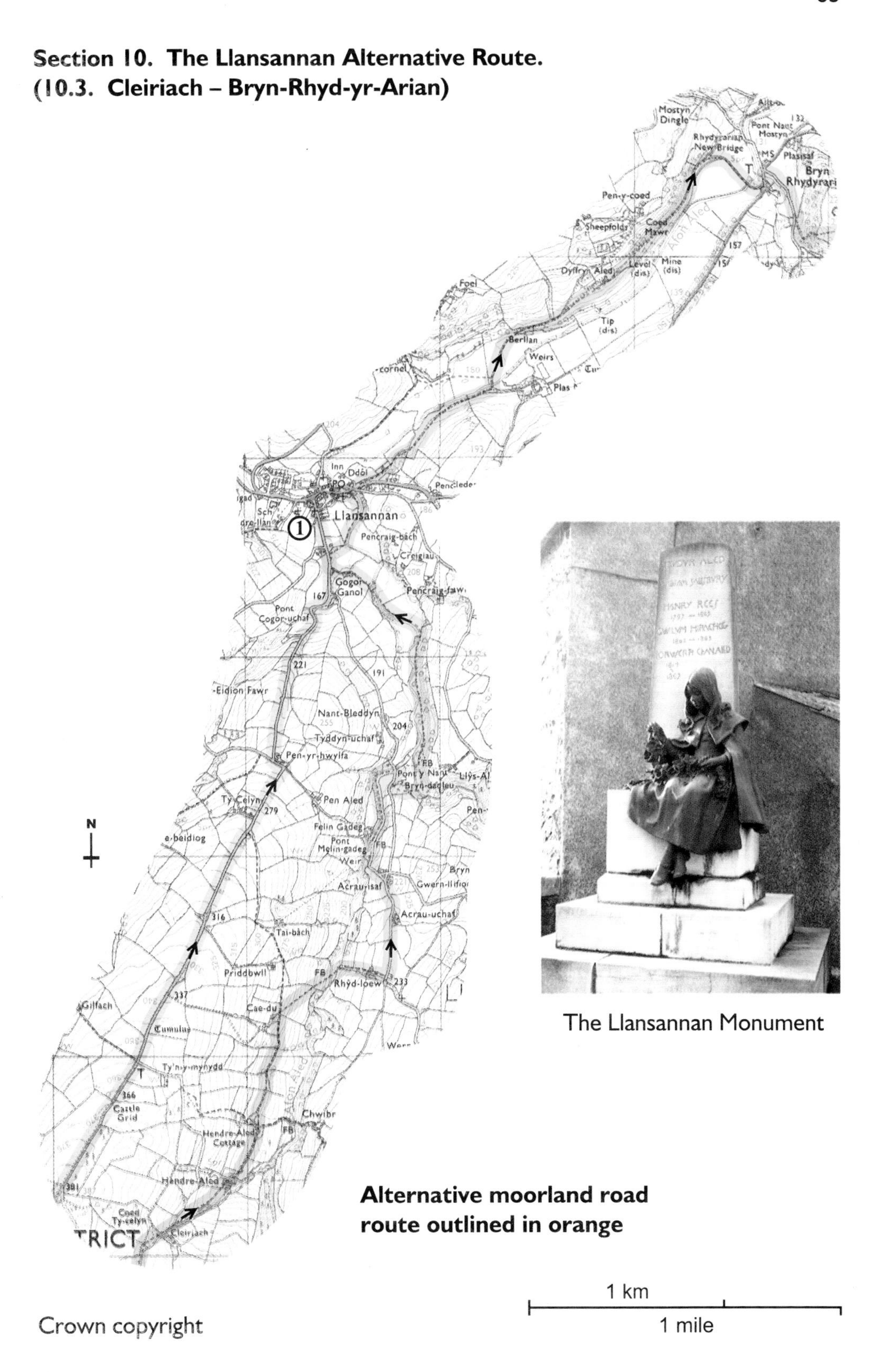


The Llansannan Monument

**Alternative moorland road route outlined in orange**

1 km
1 mile

## Section 10. The Llansannan Alternative Route.
## (10.4. Bryn-Rhyd-yr-Arian – Henllan)

**The route.** At Bryn cross over the small road bridge, then turn sharp right, taking the small side lane which runs due south. After about a quarter of a mile, however, take the footpath on the left which runs through the woods, then past Bwrdd Arthur, Coed Arllwyd, and on to Arllwyd. Here pass through the farmyard, then bear left, down the farm track to the B5382 at SH975670. Turn right here, continuing east along the road past Pont Pengwern, and on to the side lane and the old chapel at SH982673.

Turn left at this junction, taking this side lane north past Groesffordd, and on to the foot of Moel Fodiar. Here bear right, continuing round the east side of the hill to the junction with another lane at Bwlch-y-ddaugae (SH984682). Turn right here, then, after a few hundred yards, take the path on the right, which continues to the east, past Plas-coch, then on through Hafod Wood, and down to the side lane near Llechryd at SJ009686. Turn right now and follow the lane for 1 mile down to Henllan. (1)

**(1) Henllan.** The attractive village of Henllan was once the centre of a very large parish, 15 miles in length, and in some parts more than seven wide, which extended from St. Asaph, in the north-east, to the source of the river Alwen, near Llanrwst, but it was divided into more manageable proportions in 1855. Before this division about six thousand acres of 'waste land' lay within its limits, together with an adjacent two thousand acres which, together, formed a tract called 'Denbigh Green', all of which was enclosed under an Act of Parliament obtained in 1802.

The church, dedicated to St. Sadwrn, was remodelled c1806–8. The new structure occupies the site of the older church. The tower, a massive square building, which was always detached, stands on the summit of the rock adjoining the road, and at some distance away from the church. The reason given for this unusual arrangement is that it was placed there so that its bells might be heard over a greater area!

The Church, Henllan

## Section 10. The Llansannan Alternative Route.
## (10.4. Bryn-Rhyd-yr-Arian – Henllan)

Slow down when leaving Henllan!

The Church Tower, Henllan

## Section 10. The Llansannan Alternative Route.
## (10.5. Henllan – Pont Parc Canol, near Denbigh)

**The route.** From the B5382, on the east side of Henllan, and just before the school, take a side lane on the right which leads south-east up to the path which runs past the ancient ruins of Foxhall Newydd and on to Foxhall at SJ033674. (1) From Foxhall continue to the south-east, past Coed Coppy, and down to the B5382 at SJ041670. Turn sharp right here, then left, and continue due south down the path, past Lodge Farm, and on to the A543 at SJ043660. Cross over the main road and take the path, almost opposite, which leads down to Galch Hill. Turn left here then, after a few yards, take the next path on the left, which leads north-east into the south side of Denbigh.

Turn left along the minor road at the end of this path, then first right, which side road runs down to the main road by the south-west corner of Denbigh Castle. Now take the path opposite, which runs through the woods below the castle. At SJ053658 take the path south-east on the right which leads to a junction of paths at SJ055656. From here take the centre path which runs eastwards to the road at Pont Felin-ganol. Now take the path directly ahead which runs north-east under the dismantled railway, up a side lane, then under the A525, to a point near the Brookhouse at SJ072657. From here the riverside path leads past Brookhouse Farm and on to the main Denbigh–Llandyrnog road, at Pont Parc Canol, near the River Clwyd, and the 'Link-Path' connecting the northbound and southbound routes of the Clwydian Way.

**(1) Foxhall Newydd and Foxhall.** The rather spooky, ivy-clad ruin of Foxhall Newydd is all that is left, or to be more precise, all that ever existed, of an imposing mansion planned, but never completed, by John Panton, one-time Recorder of Denbigh. Clearly designed to impress, John's far from modest aim seems to have been to surpass the old Foxhall, for the building is very high, having three storeys plus a basement, and large windows in the gables. The figures 1608, over a fireplace, dates the structure very precisely. Unfortunately, Panton met with a serious cash-flow crisis, went bankrupt, and was thus obliged to swallow his pride and sell what little was completed to the Lloyds, of Foxhall, whose more ancient mansion he had hoped to eclipse! Old Foxhall was originally the residence of the celebrated antiquary, Humphrey Llwyd, who died there and was buried at Whitchurch.

## Section 10. The Llansannan Alternative Route. (10.5. Henllan – Pont Parc Canol, near Denbigh)

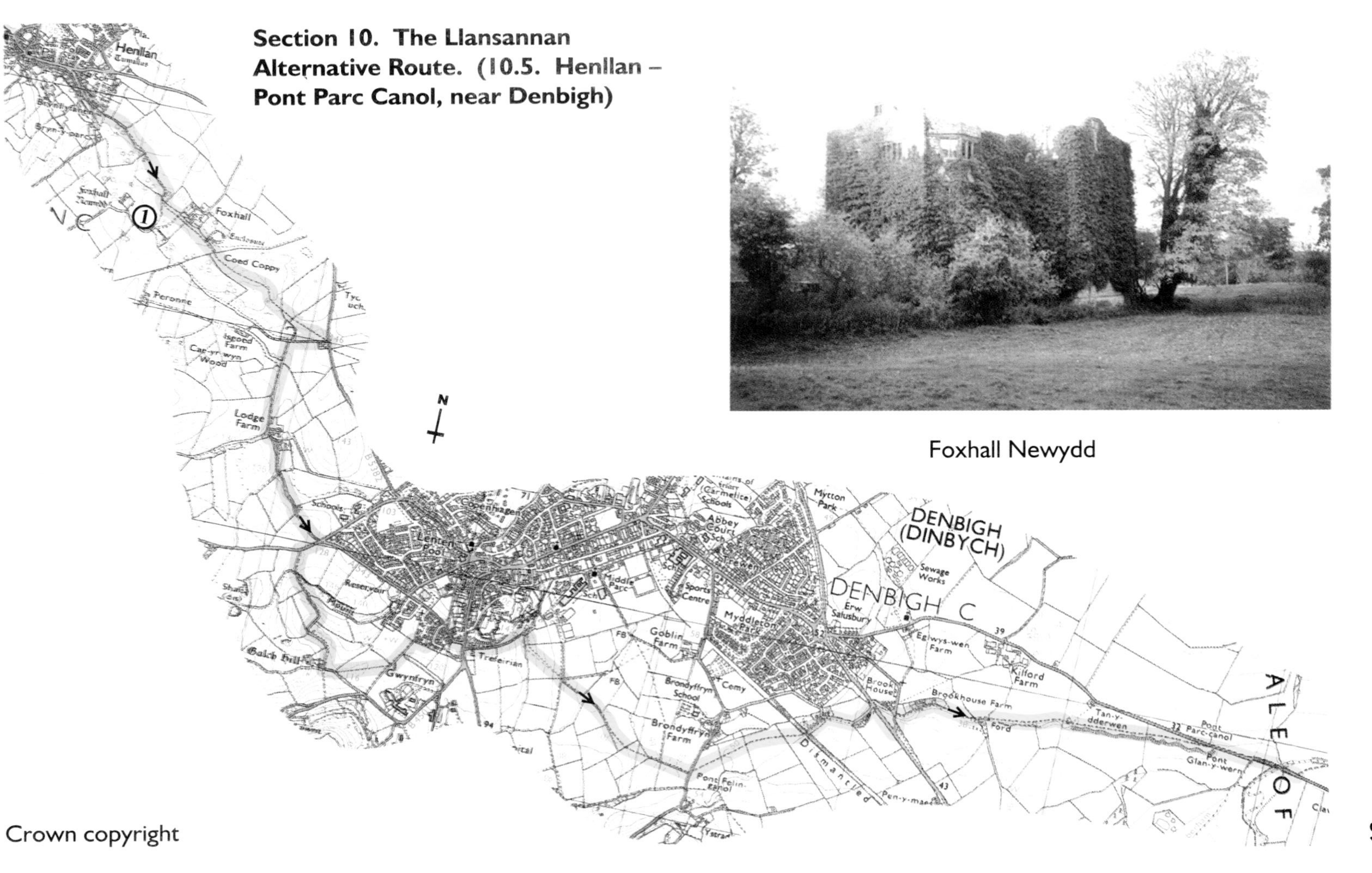


Foxhall Newydd

## Section 11. The Clwydian Way 'Link Path'. 3 miles.
## (11.1. Afon Clwyd, near Glan-y-wern farm – Fron-dyffryn, near Llangwyfan)

**The route.** The 'Link Path' is a very short, 3 mile route, running from the north-bound section of the main Clwydian Way at SJ095663 on the banks of the Clwyd, through to the south-bound section of the Clwydian Way just east of Llangwyfan, at SJ130664. From the Clwyd end take the path which leads to the lane at Pentre Bach. From here continue straight ahead up the lane to the 'T' junction on the B5429 at SJ108671. Turn right here and head south down the main road to the bend in the road at Bancar (SJ110666). Here take the path which runs south-east through the farmyard, across the next lane, then up to the west side of Llangwyfan. On the Llandyrnog–Nannerch road, at the east side of the village, turn left and proceed up the hill to the main southbound route of the Clwydian Way at SJ130664.

Denbigh

## Section 11. The Clwydian Way 'Link Path'.
## (11.1. Afon Clwyd, near Glan-y-wern farm – Fron-dyffryn, near Llangwyfan)

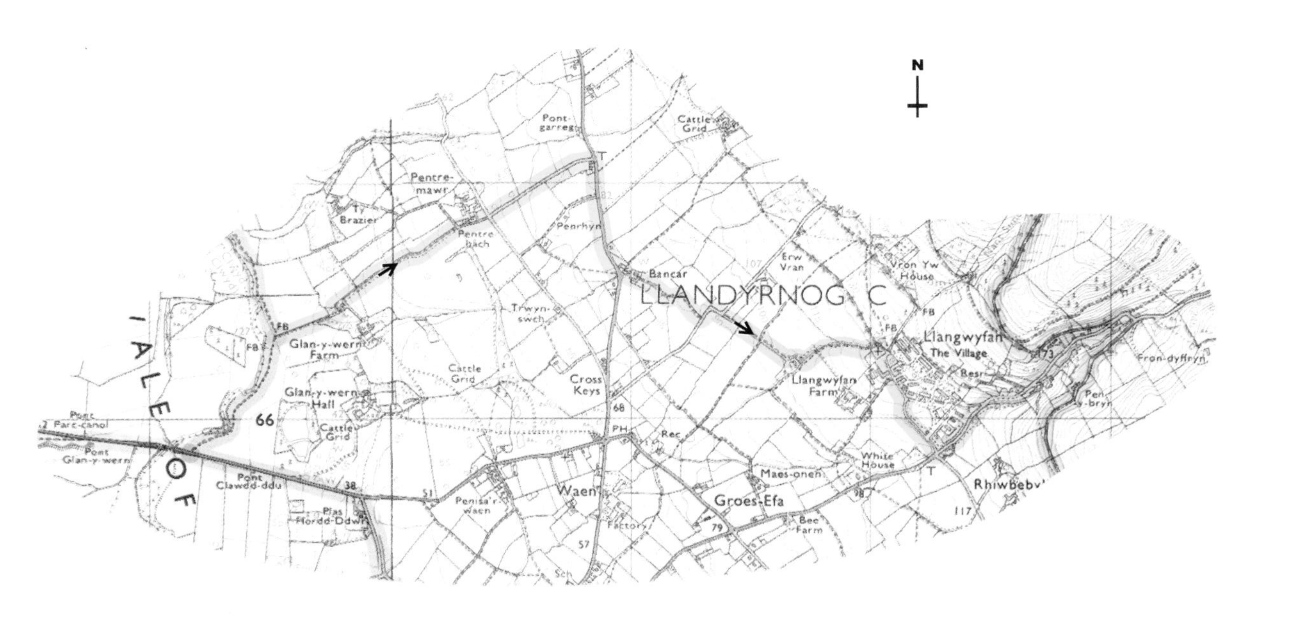


(1) Link Path outlined in yellow
(2) Main Route outlined in orange
(3) Alternative Route outlined in purple

## LOCATION MAP OF THE TWELVE SHORT CIRCULAR WALKS

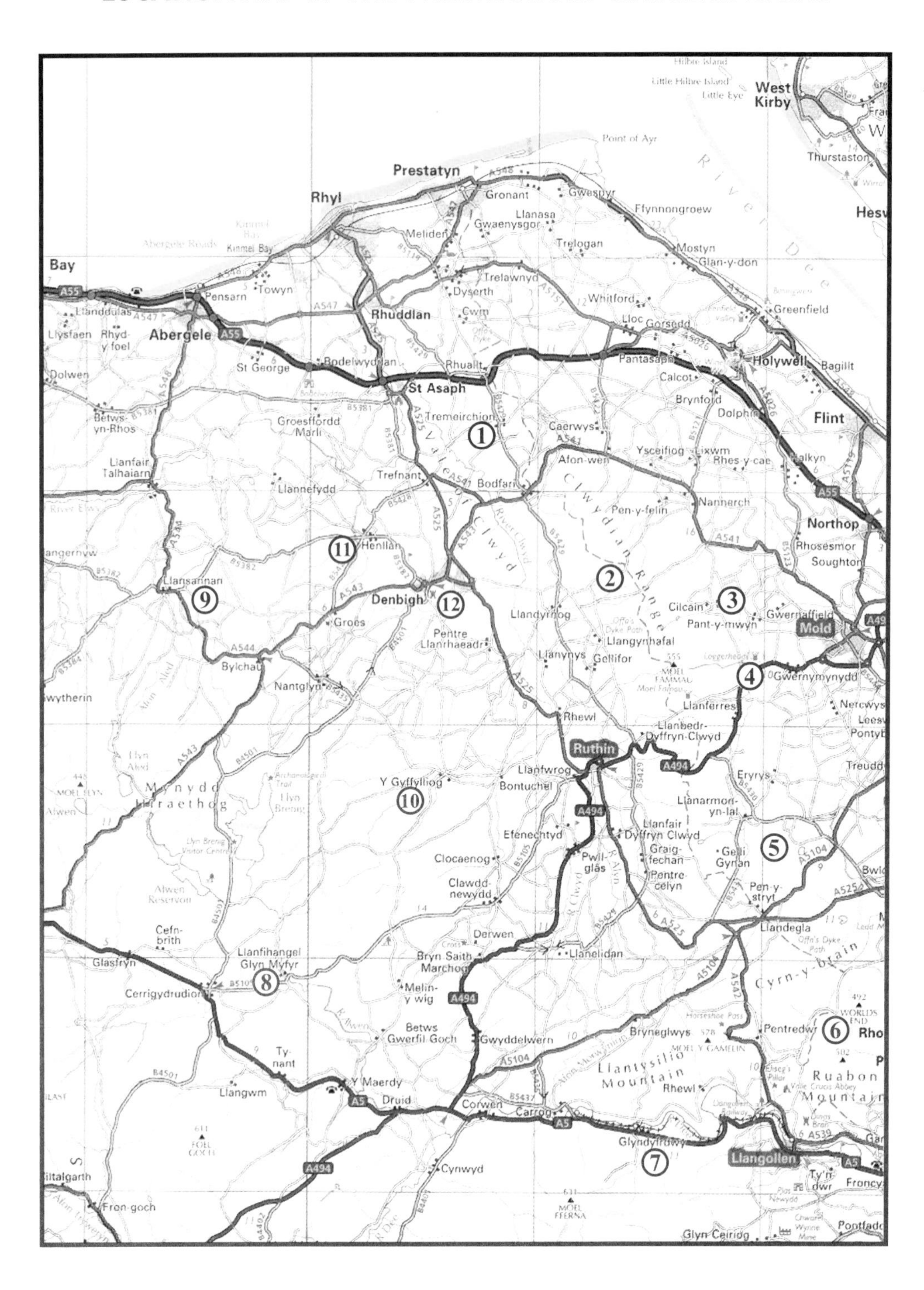

# PART 2

## THE CLWYDIAN WAY

## TWELVE SHORT CIRCULAR WALKS IN (OR NEAR) DENBIGHSHIRE, NORTH WALES

| The Walks | | Miles |
|---|---|---|
| Walk 1 | Tremeirchion | 5 |
| Walk 2 | Moel Arthur – Penycloddiau | 7 |
| Walk 3 | Cilcain – Moel Famau | 5 |
| Walk 4 | Loggerheads – Maeshafn - Pant-du | 7 |
| Walk 5 | Graianrhyd – Bod Idris Hall | 5 |
| Walk 6 | World's End – Eglwyseg Glen | 5 |
| Walk 7 | Glyndyfrdwy | 5 |
| Walk 8 | Llanfihangel Glyn Myfyr | 5 |
| Walk 9 | Llansannan | 4 |
| Walk 10 | Cyffylliog | 5 |
| Walk 11 | Henllan – Denbigh | 5 |
| Walk 12 | Denbigh – Lleweni Hall | 7 |

## SHORT CIRCULAR WALK 1. TREMEIRCHION

**Distance: 5 miles**

**Start.** Begin at the Salusbury Arms Tremeirchion. To get there take the A541 Mold–Denbigh Road to Bodfari, then take the B5429 up to the village.

**Grid Ref. SJ084730** (Pathfinder 755. Explorer 264. 265.)

**The route.** From the Salusbury Arms, Tremeirchion, follow the main route (2.1. page 14) south to the cross roads at Sodom (SJ096714). Now take the lane north, past Sodom Covert, then follow the Offa's Dyke Path, lanes, and bridleways, as outlined, back to St. Bueno's College, below Moel Maenefa. From the college follow the main route south again (1.3. page 12) back to Tremeirchion.

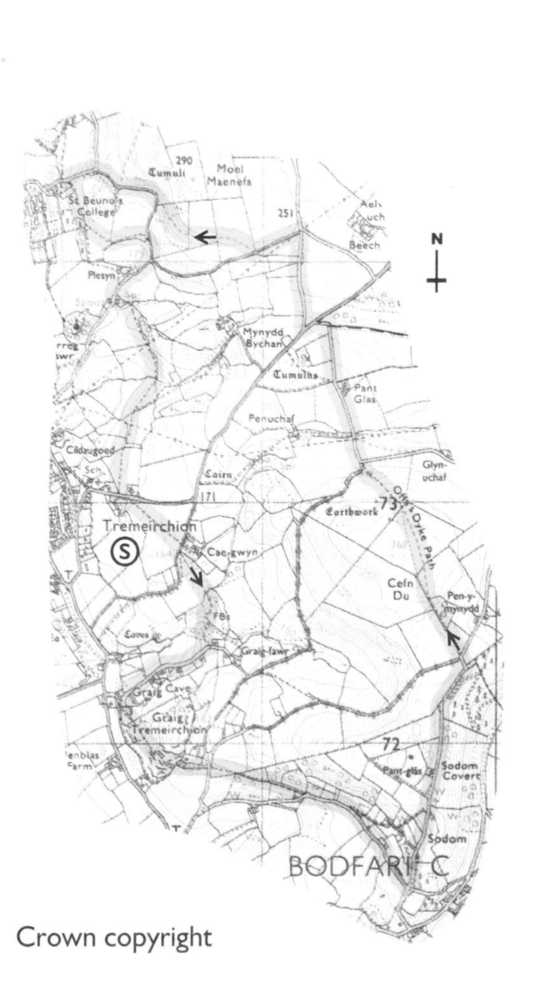

The gardens, Dinorben Arms, Bodfari

## SHORT CIRCULAR WALK 2. MOEL ARTHUR – PENYCLODDIAU

**Distance: 7 miles**

**Start.** Begin at the car park at the head of the pass between Moel Arthur and Moel Llys-y-coed. From Mold take the A541 Denbigh road. Go past the lane on the left leading to Cilcain, then take the next lane on the left at SJ173679, which leads through to Moel Arthur, and on to Llandyrnog.

**Grid Ref. SJ146657.** (Pathfinder 772. Explorer 264.265)

**The route.** From the car park near Moel Arthur take the Offa's Dyke path northbound, as outlined, over Penycloddiau, and down to the junction of path and bridleway at Nant Coed-y-mynydd (SJ121689). Now turn left, taking the main Clwydian Way route back to the car park at Moel Arthur, as outlined. ( 2.1 page 14 & 2.2. page 16)

## SHORT CIRCULAR WALK 3. CILCAIN – MOEL FAMAU

**Distance: 5 miles**

**Start.** Begin at the White Horse Inn, Cilcain. From Mold take the A541 road through Hendre and on to the junction at SJ175678. Turn left here and head south into Cilcain.

**Grid Ref. SJ177652** (Pathfinder 772. Explorer 265)

**The route.** From the White Horse Inn take the lane up to the church. Turn left at this point then take the long bridleway past the small reservoirs and on to the Offa's Dyke path at SJ145641. Now turn left, taking the ODP to the Jubilee Tower on the summit of Moel Famau. From the summit take the route, as outlined, which runs down the north side of the mountain and continues up the lane back into Cilcain.

Jubilee Monument on Moel Famau to commemorate the 50th year of the reign of George the Third, 1809

## SHORT CIRCULAR WALK 4. MAESHAFN – PANT DU

**Distance: 7 miles**

**Start.** Begin at the Loggerheads Country Park. From Mold take the A494 Ruthin road to Cadole, then continue down the hill to the Country Park.

**Grid Ref. SJ197624.** (Pathfinder 772. 773. 789. 788. Explorer 265.)

**The route.** From Loggerheads follow the main Clwydian Way route (3.1. & 3.2. pages 18 & 22) through Maeshafn and on to the lane at Pant-du (SJ206594). Now head to the west down the bridleway to SJ194595, then turn right and take the path north, past Mount Pleasant and on to the lane just below Maeshafn. Turn left here, and head down the hill to the bridge over the Afon Alun at SJ193611. Now take the path on the right which runs through the 'Fairy Glen' and on to the main A494 just to the west of Loggerheads.

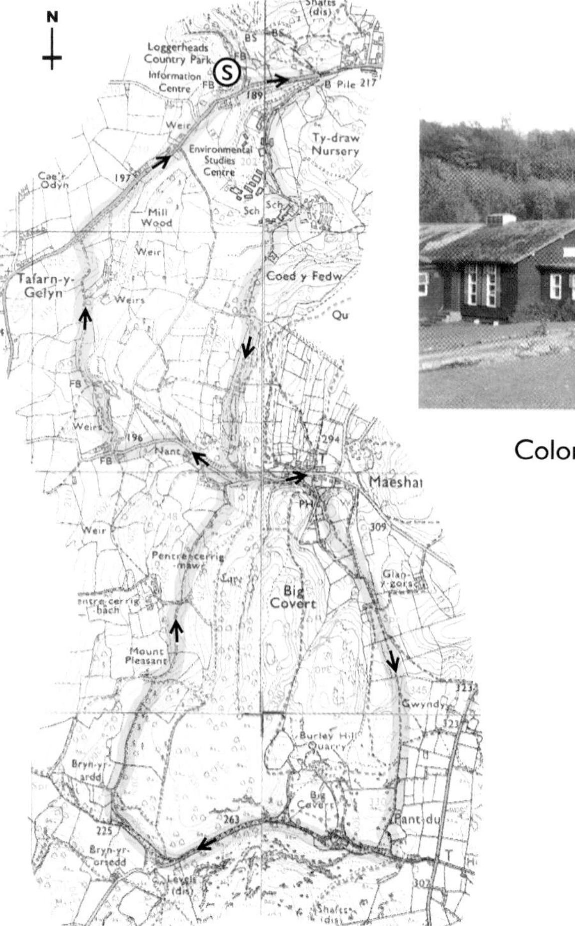


Colomendy Centre for Outdoor Education

## SHORT CIRCULAR WALK 5. GRAIANRHYD – BOD IDRIS HALL

**Distance: 5 miles**

**Start.** Graianrhyd. From the A483 expressway at Wrexham (SJ312503) take the B5430 through Coedpoeth and Rhydtalog then on to Graianrhyd.

**Grid Ref. SJ218561.** (Pathfinder 789. Explorer 256)

**The route.** From Graianrhyd take the bridleway then path which head south past Llyn Cyfynwy and on to the A5104 at SJ220541. Turn right, then take the path on the right which leads down to Gwernol. Turn right again and take the path/drive which leads up to Bod Idris Hall. From the hall continue north along the outlined route back to the starting point at Graianrhyd.

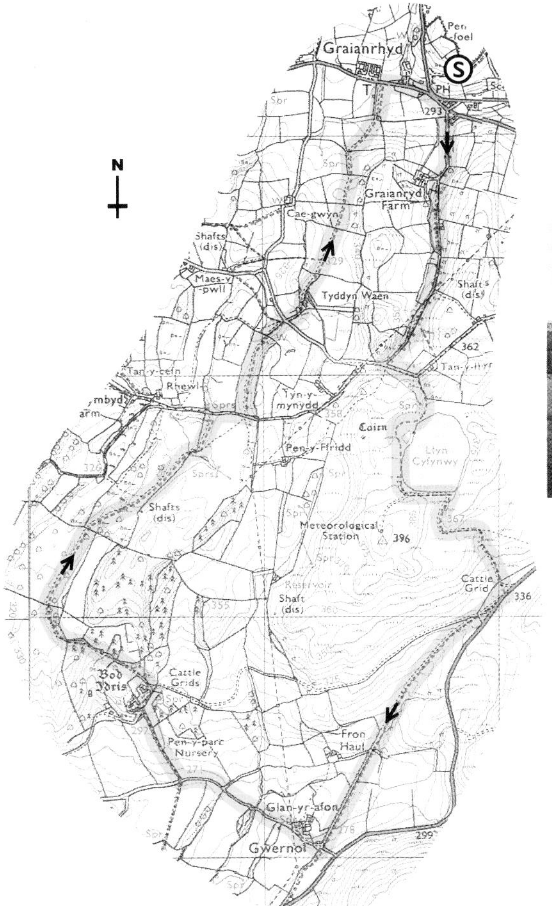

Rose and Crown, Graianrhyd

## SHORT CIRCULAR WALK 6. EGLWYSEG GLEN

**Distance: 5 miles**

**Start.** The new car park at World's End. To get there from Llangollen take the A542 Ruthin road. One mile after passing Valle Crucis Abbey take the lane on the right which is sign-posted through to World's End. The car park is just to the north of the ford at World's End, on the left-hand side, at the top of the hill.

**Grid Ref. SJ232483.** (Pathfinder 806. Explorer 256.)

**The route.** This walk passes through some of the most spectacular country in North Wales. From the car park head down the lane towards the ford at World's End, then continue down the lane, past the old Manor House, to the bend in the lane at Ty Canol (SJ221475). Turn right here and follow the track, as outlined, past Pant Glas and Glyn, then down to Plas Yn Eglwyseg, Eglwyseg Glen, at SJ216462. Take the small link path over to the Offa's Dyke Path, then turn left and follow this trail, below the great cliffs of Craig Arthur, back to the car park.

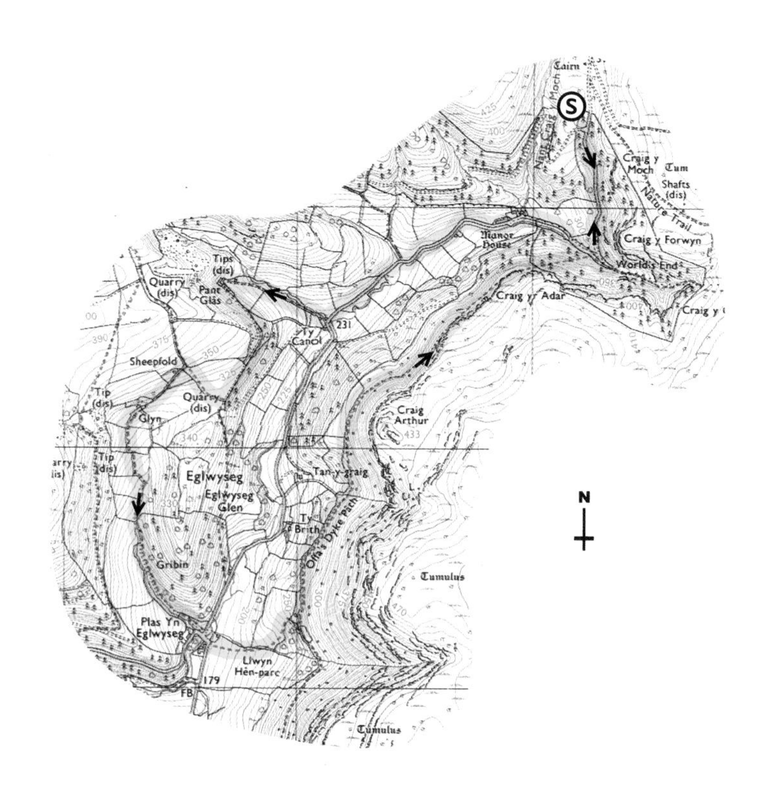

Eglwyseg Rocks

The Old Manor House, World's End

## SHORT CIRCULAR WALK 7. GLYNDYFRDWY

**Distance: 5 miles**

**Start.** Glyndyfrdwy, 4 miles to the west of Llangollen on the A5 Holyhead road.

**Grid Ref. SJ152426.** (Pathfinder 805. Explorer 255. 256)

**The route.** From the A5 take the small lane by the church which heads south towards the Ceiriog Forest then, after a few hundred yards, take the path on the left, which runs past Siamber Wen and Dreboeth, through Coed Ty'n-y-graig and out on to the open moorland. When the path meets the 'county road' at SJ148396 (just on Pathfinder 826), turn right and head back down the hill, taking the route as outlined.

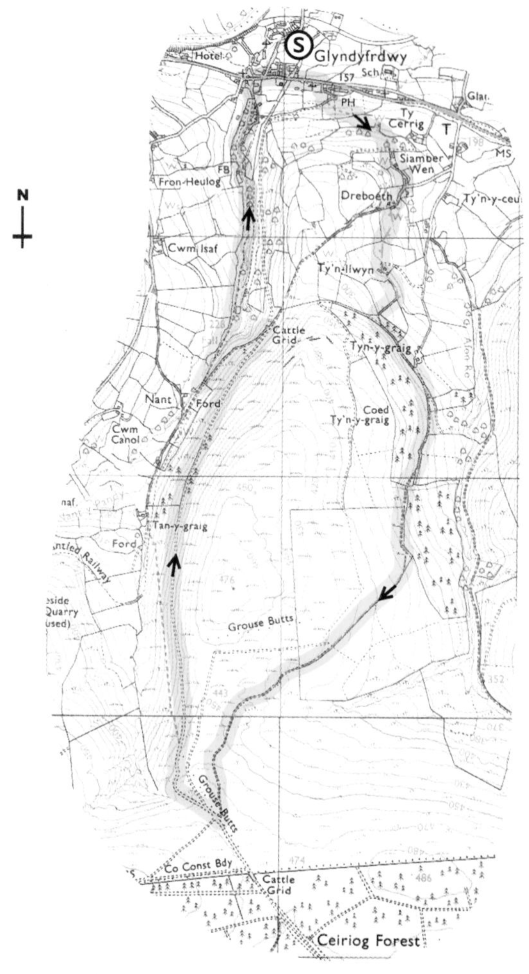

## SHORT CIRCULAR WALK 8. LLANFIHANGEL GLYN MYFYR

**Distance: 5 miles**

**Start.** Llanfihangel Glyn Myfyr, 10 miles south-west of Ruthin on the B5105 Ruthin–Cerrigydrudion Road.

**Grid Ref. SH991491.** (Pathfinder 787. Explorer 264)

**The route.** From the Crown Inn, Llanfihangel, follow the main Clwydian Way route (6.3 page 40) through to the Afon Alwen at SH989518. Now turn left, taking the path along the east bank of the river to the footbridge at SH987510. From this point follow the lane due south back to the Crown Inn, Llanfihangel.

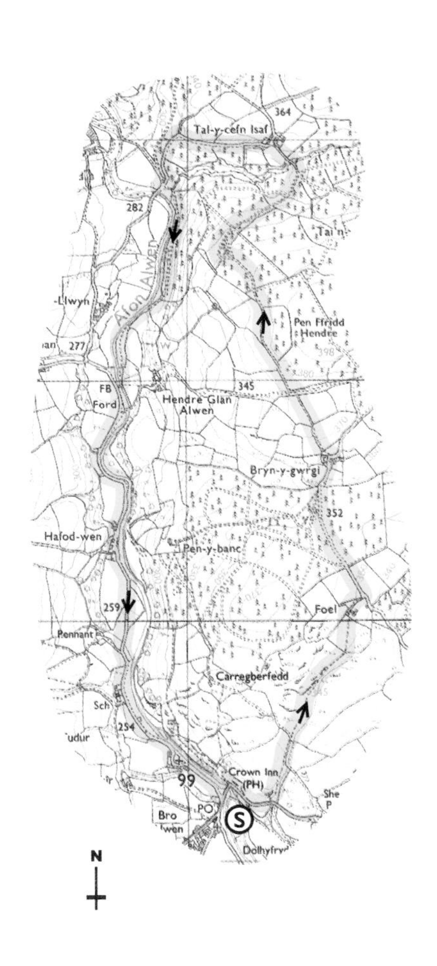

The Bridge, Llanfihangel Glyn Myfyr

## SHORT CIRCULAR WALK 9. LLANSANNAN

**Distance: 4 miles**

**Start.** Llansannan, on the A544. From Abergele (on the A55 coastal express-way) take the A548 to Llanfair Talhaiarn, then the A544 to Llansannan.

**Grid Ref. SH934658.** Pathfinder 771, Explorer 264)

**The route.** From the village take the road leading due south to Llyn Aled. At Gogol Ganol bear left and continue along this lane to Pont y Nant at SH937644. Here take the path on the right which runs along the east side of the Afon Aled to Pont Melin-gadeg. Now follow the lanes back to Pont y Nant, but before crossing over the bridge take the path on the right which runs through the woods back to the road at Gogol Ganol. After about 100 yards take the path on the right which leads through to the east side of Llansannan. Cross over the road and continue along the riverside path to SH943663, which is just to the west of Plas Newydd. Now return to Llansannan along the path which runs past Plas-yn-cornel, on the north side of the river.

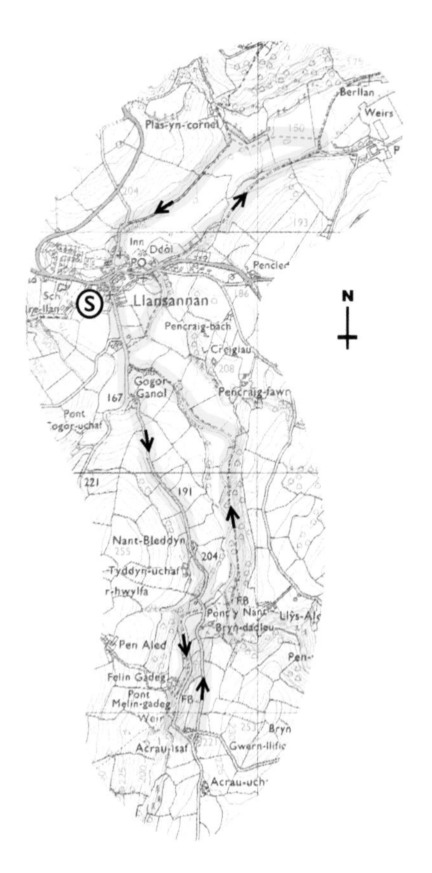

The Afon Aled, Llansannan

## SHORT CIRCULAR WALK 10. CYFFYLLIOG

**Distance: 5 miles**

**Start.** Cyffylliog, on the Afon Clywedog. From Ruthin take the B5105 road out of town; however, just after leaving Ruthin take the road on the right, sign-posted Bontuchel and Cyffylliog.

**Grid Ref. SJ060577.** (Pathfinder 788. Explorer 264)

**The route.** Leave the village by taking the small lane which runs along the south side of the Afon Clywedog then, at the point marked 'Ford', cross over the river by the footbridge and continue along the north bank of the river to the lane at SJ035594. Turn right here, then right again, following the hill-top lane due east to Carreg-y-gath at SJ057594. Take the lane on the right, then the path on the left which leads back down the hill to another lane just to the north-east of Cyffylliog.

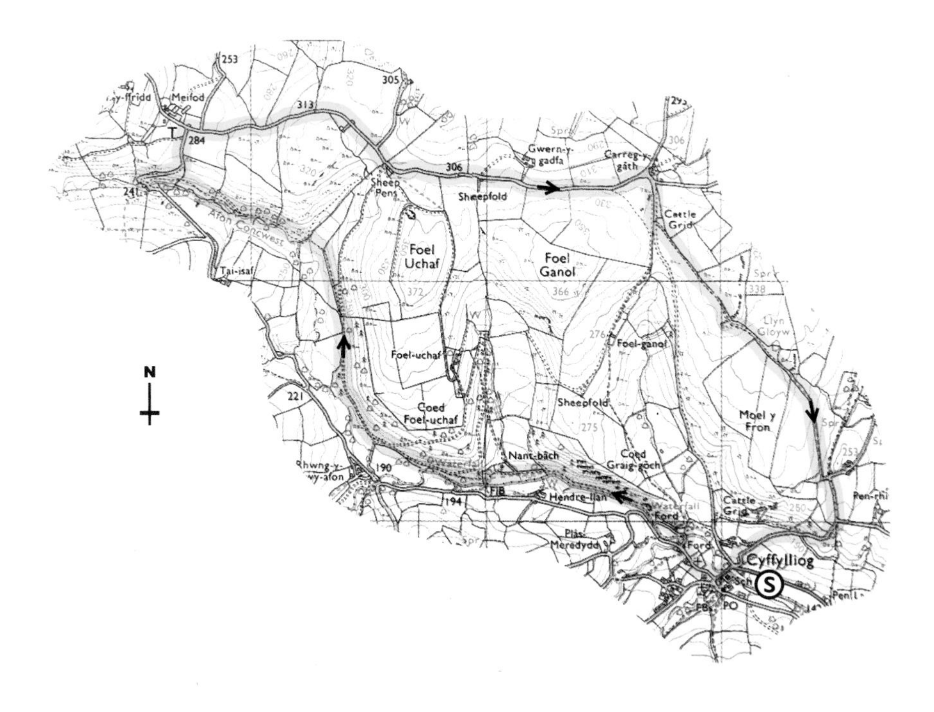

## SHORT CIRCULAR WALK 11. HENLLAN – DENBIGH

**Distance: 5 miles**

**Start.** From Denbigh take the B5382 to Henllan. The walk starts on the main road near the village school.

**Grid Ref. SJ026681.** (Pathfinder 772. Explorer 264)

**The route.** From Henllan follow the directions on the main (alternative) route of the Clwydian Way (10.5. page 68) down to the A543 at SJ043660 by Denbigh. Turn left here, taking the main road down the hill to the junction with the B5382. Now take the path which runs between Coppy Farm and Copenhagen, past Crest Mawr, and over Denbigh Golf Course to a side lane at SJ042681. Turn left, continue along the lane, then take the 1st left, then turn right taking the B5382 back to Henllan.

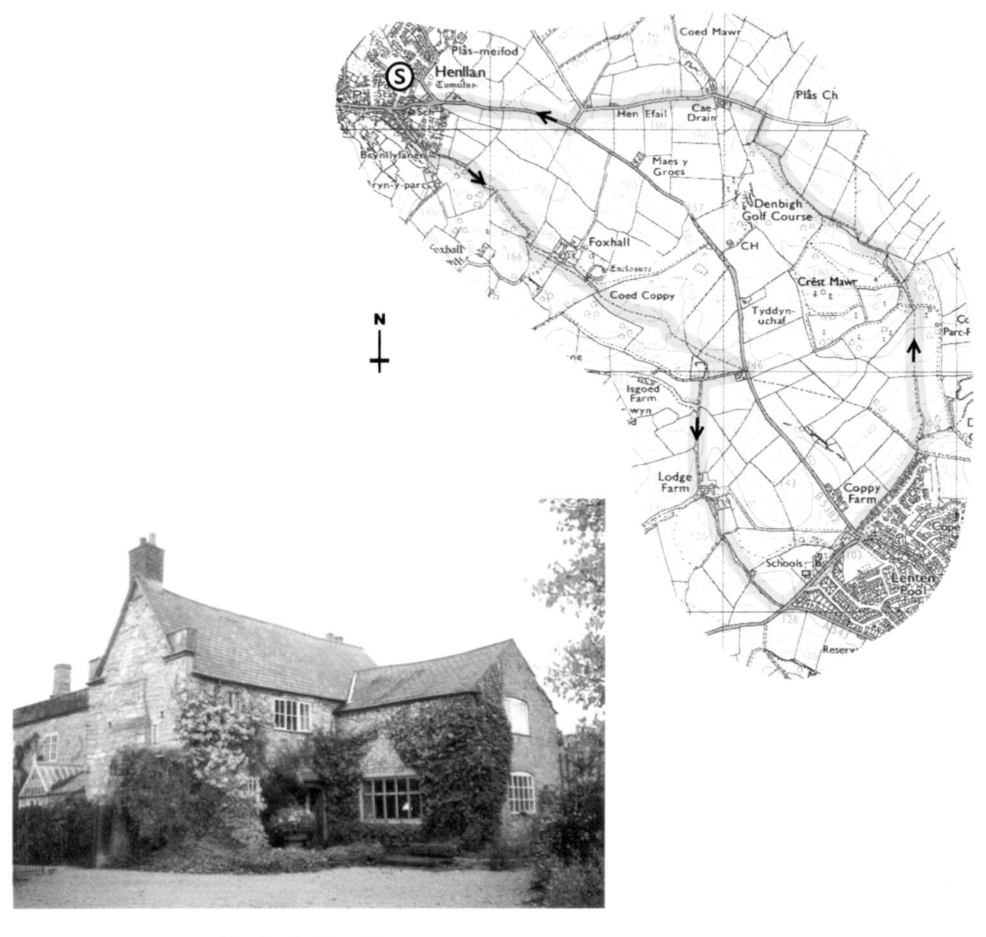


Foxhall, Henllan

## SHORT CIRCULAR WALK 12. DENBIGH – LLEWENI HALL

**Distance: 7 miles**

**Start.** By the roundabout on the A525, Denbigh, near Erw Salusbury.

**Grid Ref. SJ067661.** (Pathfinder 772. Explorer 264.)

**The route.** From the roundabout near Erw Salusbury take the A525 down to the Brookhouse pub. Now take the path which runs along the bank of a stream to Pont Parc-canal on the Denbigh–Llandyrnog road. Turn right, cross over the Clwyd road bridge, then take the path on the left which heads north to Lleweni Hall, along the east bank of the river. Return to Denbigh via the farm road/bridleway which runs down to Kilford Farm near Denbigh.

**Please note.** The path along the banks of the River Clwyd, near Lleweni Hall, is subject to flooding during winter months.

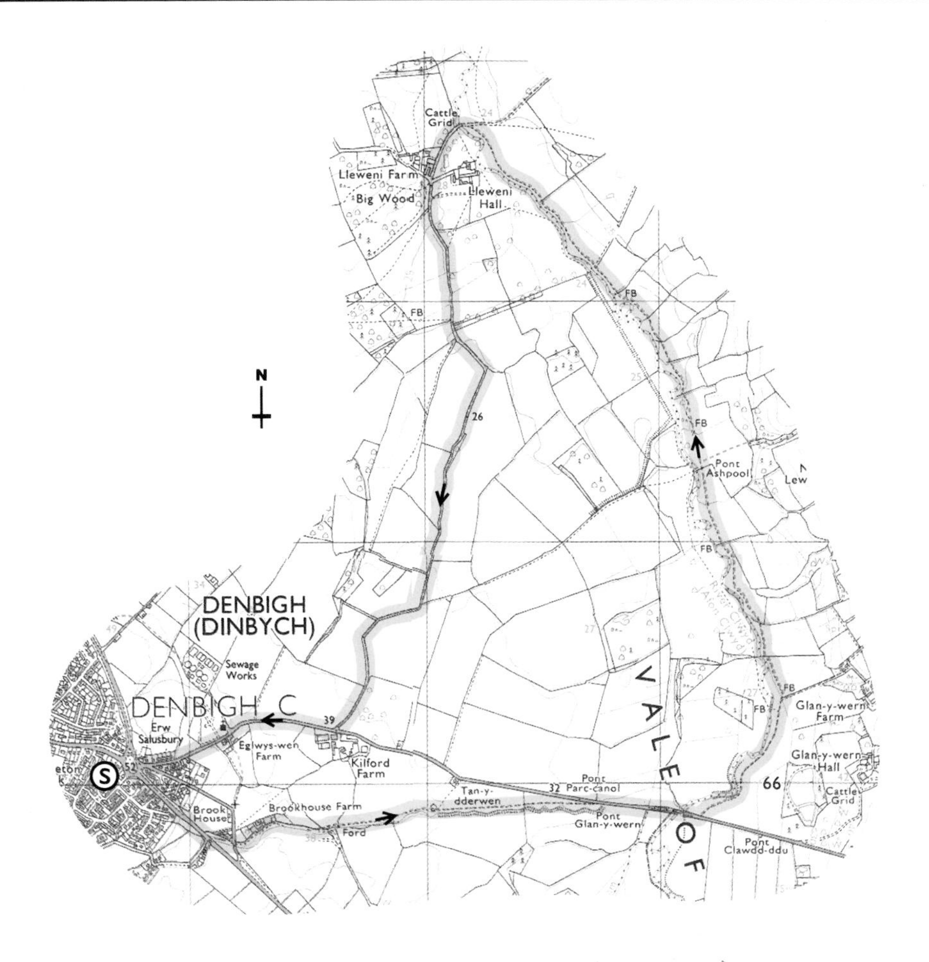

# NOTES

# NOTES

# NOTES